PENINSULA PORTRAIT

Peninsula Portrait

An Illustrated History of San Mateo County
by Mitchell P. Postel
Picture Research by Sandi Tatman
"Partners in Progress" by Katherine C. Feallock

Produced in cooperation with the
San Mateo County Historical Association

Windsor Publications, Inc.
Northridge, California

Windsor Publications, Inc.—
History Book Division

Vice President, Publishing:
Hal Silverman

Editorial Director:
Teri Davis Greenberg

Design Director:
Alexander D'Anca

Corporate Biographies Director:
Karen Story

Staff for *Peninsula Portrait*

Editor:
Lane A. Powell

Photo Editor:
Lynne Ferguson Chapman

Assistant Director,
Corporate Biographies:
Phyllis Gray

Editor, Corporate Biographies:
Brenda Berryhill

Editorial Assistants:
Didier Beauvoir, Thelma Fleischer, Kathy B.
Peyser, Pat Pittman, Theresa Solis

Proofreader:
Susan J. Muhler

Sales Representative,
Corporate Biographies:
Gina Woolf

Layout Artist, Corporate Biographies:
Mari Catherine Preimesberger

Designer:
Ellen Ifrah

Library of Congress Cataloging-in-Publication data:

Postel, Mitchell.
Peninsula portrait.

"Produced in cooperation with the San Mateo County Historical Association."
Bibliography:
Includes index.
1. San Mateo County (Calif.)—History. 2. San Mateo County (Calif.)—Description and travel—Views. 3. San Mateo County (Calif.)—Industries. I. San Mateo County (Calif.)—Industries. I. San Mateo County Historical Association. II. Title.
F868.S19P69 1988 979.4'69 87-27928
ISBN 0-89781-255-7

Published 1988
Printed in the United States of America
First Edition

CONTENTS

INTRODUCTION

Like most histories, this illustrated history of San Mateo County is derived from written histories that preceded it. In fact, most of the research for this book was not dredged from primary source materials such as memoirs, letters, and documents. Instead, it relies heavily on the writings of an assortment of scholars. Over the years San Mateo County is lucky to have had so many capable and productive local historians who took its history seriously. Their work has made the job of creating this volume a pleasurable chore.

The first histories written about San Mateo County are commonly referred to as "mug books." A variety of publishing firms undertook these works during the last three decades of the nineteenth century and first four decades of the twentieth century. Various leading citizens in the county sponsored their creation. The mug books contained a narrative section that covered the general history of the county. They also detailed the biographies of the sponsors, and photographs of these individuals often were included with the biographies. The name "mug book," which came from the slang word "mug" (for face), derived from the portraits appearing on the pages of the texts. The value of these original histories is great. Many of the scholarly works that followed used them as at least a point of departure for further study. The biographies of the sponsors continue to be of tremendous value. Many of the county's early pioneers and important citizens can be found in mug books and nowhere else. It is interesting that the book you are reading has returned to this kind of format, only instead of highlighting sponsoring individuals, it focuses on businesses.

In 1937 Arthur H. Cawston, a publisher of local histories, commissioned

The southern portion of the peninsula retained its rural character well into the twentieth century. This photo shows a stretch of El Camino Real in present-day Atherton, about 1905. At the time it was still an unpaved country road, but today it has four to six lanes and is the peninsula's major thoroughfare, flanked by businesses and office buildings. Photo by W.E. Worden. Courtesy, Worden Collection, San Mateo County Historical Association Archives

Dr. Frank M. Stanger to write one of the last of the San Mateo County mug books. This brought onto the scene a prolific scholar whose written works, classroom instruction, and community leadership gave a whole new meaning to local history. Over a span of 25 years, Stanger wrote three general histories of San Mateo County, the last of which, *South From San Francisco* (1963), is still extremely popular. He additionally authored two books about specific aspects of the county's history, and wrote countless articles for the San Mateo County Historical Association, which he also served as third president and first curator. Besides his research and writing activities, Stanger founded the local history class at the College of San Mateo, and under his leadership the campus history museum was created. Stanger also spearheaded the preservation of landmark buildings in the county and was responsible for gaining recognition for many local historic sites.

Stanger came to San Mateo County intellectually well-equipped for these duties. He spent five years (1920-1925) in Lima, Peru, earning a Doctor en Historia from the Universidad Mayor de San Marcos. This not only prepared him for the study of history but gave him the ability to translate the accounts and documents of the Spanish explorers, missionaries, and rancho owners applicable to the peninsula. In 1930 he received his Ph.D. from the University of California at Berkeley, where he studied under the eminent historian, Herbert Eugene Bolton.

Almost 20 years passed between the time that Stanger published *South From San Francisco* and the appearance of another general history about the county. In 1982 Dr. Alan Hynding completed *From Frontier to Suburb*. Hynding, whose grandfather, Andrew Hynding, had been the first mayor of South San Francisco, had a great love for local history. He earned his Ph.D. from the University of Washington and began to teach in 1967 at the College of San Mateo, where he succeeded Stanger as local history instructor. For 10 years he gathered materials for his new study. Hynding's history concentrates on land use changes, population patterns, politics, twentieth-century developments, and other topics not explored in depth by Stanger. Taken together, *South From San Francisco* and *From Frontier to Suburb* cover the history of San Mateo County in a masterful way. They provided much of the material for this book, although other sources have also had a major impact.

Chapter 1 is an excellent example. Neither Stanger nor Hynding expended much energy on the local Indians, perhaps feeling that this subject was more in the realm of anthropology. Only Alan K. Brown, a Stanford graduate student who collaborated with Stanger on a variety of projects, took a careful look at the native people of the peninsula as a historian in his comprehensive article in *La Peninsula* (Winter 1973-1974), the journal of the San Mateo County Historical Association.

In order to further understand what our local Indians were like, one also has to review the works of anthropologists. Of value for the completion of this book were Alfred L. Krober's monumental *Handbook of the Indians of California* (1925), Robert F. Heizer's *The Costanoan Indians* (1974), Richard Levy's chapter, "The Costanoans," from the series, *Handbook of North American Indians* (1978), and, most of all, Malcolm Margolin's sensitive and erudite *The Ohlone Way* (1978).

Chapter 2, which probes the Spanish experience, drew heavily on several sources, including the Stanger and Brown book, *Who Discovered the Golden Gate* (1969), Dr. Fernando Bonue's *Gaspar de Portola: Explorer and Founder of California* (1983), Dorothy Regnery's *Battle of Santa Clara* (1978), and an article by Shirley Drye, "Don Francisco Sanchez—A Man of Integrity," *La Peninsula* (January 1986).

Of great use for Chapter 3 were Stanger's *Sawmills in the Redwoods* (1967), Brown's *Sawpits in the Spanish Redwoods* (1966), and a variety of sources on San Francisco's Vigilance Committee of 1856, including the works of such California historians as Hubert Howe Bancroft, Josiah Royce, and Walton Bean.

Chapter 4's regional histories were aided by Sam Chandler's *Gateway to the Peninsula* (1973), Linda Kauffman's *History of South San Francisco* (1976), Don Ringler's *San Mateo, USA* (1976), Ringler and George Rossi's *Filoli* (1978), Gilbert Richard's *Crossroads* (1973), Jack R. Wagner's *The Last Whistle* (1974), and a host of *La Peninsula* articles, including Darold Fredrick's "The City of San Bruno: A Look to the Past" (December 1984), Ringler's "Hillsborough-San Mateo Mansions" (Winter 1976), and Stanger's "Redwood City" (October 1951). Also included in this chapter was original research conducted by the author on the Mid-County and bayline industries.

Chapter 5 and 6 also benefited from original research plus Barbara Simon's *A New Town Comes of Age—Foster City, California* (1985), the Japanese American Citizens League's *1872-1942: A Community Story* (1981), and Elaine Thomas' *La Peninsula* article, "The Italians in San Mateo County" (Fall 1981).

Wherever possible, additional sources are cited in the body of the narrative. A comprehensive bibliography can be found at the end of this book.

1

NATIVE AMERICANS OF THE PENINSULA

Who were the people who lived on the peninsula before the Spanish explorers arrived? About all that can be said of these people that everyone will agree on is that there is much disagreement about them. Scholars cannot even settle on a name for these Native Americans. Some prefer to use a Spanish-derived word for coastal people, "Costanoan," because it has been in use within the scholastic community the longest. Others prefer the appellation, "Ohlone," because this is the name favored by descendants of the local Indians today. The origins of this word are vague. It may have been either the name of a village along the San Mateo County coastline or a Miwok term meaning "western people."

Whether one uses Costanoan or Ohlone, all scholars agree that both

Facing page: This lithograph of Indian family life in the California missions is signed "by Norblin after Choris," indicating the artist's debt to Louis Choris, the first artist to record California's native inhabitants. Courtesy, Bancroft Library

designations are fabrications. The local Indians never referred to themselves by either term. Instead of seeing themselves as a tribe of 10,000 people, within a geographic area stretching from Contra Costa County to Monterey County, they affiliated themselves with much smaller tribelets, made up of dozens, not thousands, of people.

The Costanoan or Ohlone are classified as one group of California Indians because of linguistic similarities among the tribelets. Nevertheless, eight languages and dozens of dialects existed within the group.

Besides some similarities in speech and custom, our local Indi-

Russian artist Louis Choris accompanied Lieutenant Otto von Kotzebue on an expedition to the California coast in the late eighteenth and early nineteenth centuries. In 1822 he published a portfolio of his drawings of the Indians of the California coast. Courtesy, San Mateo County Historical Association Archives

ans had little else in common. There was never any political alliance among the tribelets, and wars occurred frequently between neighbors.

Just as there is little accord over what to call the Indians, there is much discrepancy among guesses as to when they first came to this area. Anthropologists call their ancestors the "Penutians." Some

scholars, such as Malcolm Margolin, in his book *The Ohlone Way,* place the Indians' arrival in the San Francisco Bay area at perhaps as long as 5,000 years ago. Others feel that they arrived much later than that. Richard Levy, in his chapter, "The Costanoans," in the series, *Handbook of North American Indians* (published the same year, 1978, as Margolin's book), puts the arrival of the Penutians at A.D. 500 (a 3,500-year difference!).

Why are there so many discrepancies about our local Indians? For one thing, the Ohlone (the term preferred by the author) were a prehistoric people—that is, they never developed any form of writing—and thus left no record about themselves. Scholars have gained knowledge about them through what other contemporary people have written, and the things, ranging from tools to their own bones, the Ohlone left behind.

The Spanish explorers and missionaries, who had the greatest contact with the Ohlone, are therefore looked to for analyses of the char-

acter, industry, society, and culture of this people. Unfortunately, the Spanish were disappointed with what they found. The Ohlone's lack of accumulated wealth and failure in the eyes of the missionaries to succeed in living a new life as Christians led the Spanish to believe that the Ohlone were simply a backward and lazy people, who were poor because they let anarchy prevail in their society.

This impression was a lasting one. Even those who found positive things to report about most of the California Indians could write little that was good about the Ohlone. Alfred L. Krober was a great anthropologist from the University of California who improved our knowledge of the native peoples of California significantly. He wrote in his *Handbook of California Indians* (1925) that the Costanoan were "dark, dirty, squalid and apathetic; and travelers coming from the north as well as south were struck by the obvious paucity and rudeness of the native culture in the Coastanoan area as compared with other regions."

Local historians seemed to either ignore the native peoples or agree with Krober until 1973. Toward the end of that year, Alan K. Brown, a graduate student at Stanford University and a research associate of the San Mateo County Historical Association, published an article in the association's journal, *La Peninsula* (Winter 1973-74). This article investigated the history of the native peoples who lived within the boundaries of what is known today as San Mateo County. By examining mission records and the journals of some of the explorers and missionaries, Brown gives an amazingly clear picture of the Indi-

MAGIC

THESE STONES WERE BELIEVED TO HAVE MAGIC POWERS. THE LABOR EXPENDED IN SHAPING AND POLISHING THEM IS EVIDENCE OF THEIR GREAT IMPORTANCE TO THE COSTANOS.

JEWELRY

ans once present here. He explains that the range of the Ohlone encompassed several counties and that there were at least 10 tribelets, with populations numbering between 100 and 250, in San Mateo County alone. The most heavily populated spot in the county is now underwater. Behind today's Crystal Springs Dam dwelled a tribelet known as the "Shalshon" or "Salson." Other tribelets existed in the vicinities of Pescadero, San Gregorio, Half Moon Bay, Pacifica, Redwood City, and the Belmont-San Carlos area, among other locations.

Above: This drawing portrays Indians at the Mission San Jose, just south of the present county of San Mateo. The body adornments may have had religious significance because of the Indians' spiritual attachment to nature. Courtesy, California Historical Society, San Francisco

Left: Excavations of Indian burial mounds in San Mateo County have yielded artifacts such as those shown here. Native rock was honed into arrowheads and spearpoints, and shells were used as jewelry. Courtesy, San Mateo County Historical Association Archives

In addition to Brown's work, the 1970s produced a quantity of scholarly studies about the local native peoples that culminated in Malcomb Margolin's publication *The Ohlone Way* in 1978. Margolin at last challenged every disparaging theory about these people in a book that deserves attention. His work, combined with the perspective of Robert F. Heizer in *The Costanoan Indians* (1974) and Richard Levy in "The Costanoans" (in the *Handbook of North American Indians*), gives a very different view of our local Indians.

Despite the stigma of being a backward people, before contact with the Spanish, the Ohlone, along with the other Indians of Central California, had the densest population of any Native American group north of Mexico. Of course this had much to do with the generous environment of the region. Throughout the geographic area of the Ohlone dwelled abundant animal life, which included seabirds, geese, ducks, elk, pronghorn antelope, and deer. On the bay lands there existed large quantities of shellfish, and on the coast were sea lion, seal, and beached whales. Said a French observer, "There is not any country in the world which more abounds in fish and game of every description."

Until the arrival of the Spanish, the Ohlone lived in an extremely stable world. No existing evidence suggests that they ever suffered from a major fire, flood, famine, or disease. The first Europeans saw much evidence of this stability.

Along the bay line huge shell mounds, the refuse from centuries of consumption of shellfish, were evident. Some mounds were recorded as being 30 feet deep and a quarter of a mile across. In higher areas another sign of the continuity of Ohlone life was visible. Observers noted that in spots well-used foot trails were pressed a foot and a half below the surrounding land due to constant use.

Villages were normally located close to freshwater creeks. Houses, which ranged from 6 to 20 feet in diameter, were built out of tule reeds, a marsh plant. A sweat house usually was present. The Spanish called these mud structures "temescals."

The Ohlone were hunter gatherers—they did not practice agriculture, but subsisted on what they could find in the wilds. Their diet included a large assortment of foods, from insects and lizards to

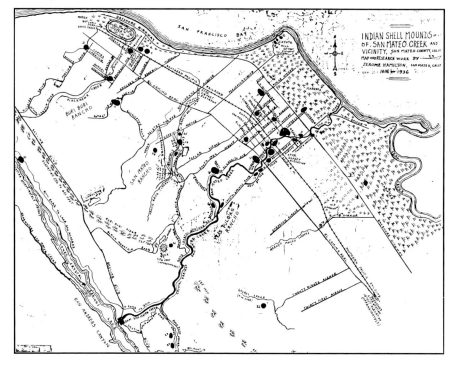

This map, drawn by James Hamilton in 1936, shows the location of Indian shell mounds in mid-county. Each mound represents an area where the nomadic Ohlone lived for a time. Preferred campgrounds were along creeks and near the bay. Courtesy, San Mateo County Historical Association Archives

deer. The great staple was the acorn, which was shucked, ground, leached, and cooked into a paste.

Ohlone men sometimes wore beards. Ears and noses were pierced, and long plugs of wood or bone were inserted. Otherwise they went naked.

The women wore skirts made of tule reeds and deerskin. Tattoos lined their faces and indicated family lineage. Sex roles were well-defined. The life of a man was taken up by hunting and fishing. The temescal was his domain, where he prepared himself spiritually for the deer hunt. After the kill, the hunter himself would not eat the meat of the deer he had brought back, out of respect for the animal and for its special place in the religious world of the Ohlone.

Women were involved with gathering food, including shellfish and acorns, preparing meals, and basket making. Women could be-

come chieftains and even shamen (religious leaders).

During the centuries that the Ohlone occupied their portion of coastal California, they kept their population constant at about 10,000 people. They did this by limiting sexual contact during ritual periods (before the hunt, during menstruation, two years after giving birth, and others). They also accepted homosexuality and practiced abortion.

The Ohlone did another thing to help control their world. From time to time they burned the land. They did this deliberately, for several important ecological reasons which indicate that this native people had a great understanding of their environment. First, the fires kept the chaparral from overrunning the meadowlands, which were important to the herds of elk, deer and antelope. Second, burning was necessary to the germination process of the digger pines, a significant source of nuts. Third, it encouraged certain grasses and flowers valued for their seeds. Finally, it prevented the buildup of combustibles, which could lead to a truly disastrous conflagration.

Thus, when the first European observers came to lands occupied by the Ohlone and remarked upon the abundance of animal life and other forms of food, they could have credited the Ohlone for this condition. By keeping a reverence for their environment through their spiritual world, curbing the growth of their own population, and periodically burning the land to their advantage, the Ohlone successfully maintained their surroundings for generation after generation.

CONTACT WITH THE EUROPEANS

Of course, the world as the Ohlone knew it was turned upside down with the arrival of the Spanish explorers and missionaries beginning in 1769. As one might expect, the initial reaction of many of the Ohlone people was fear. Seeing the Spanish with their different physical appearance, clothing, and metal weapons and tools was frightening enough. The sight of the aliens riding on animals, which were strange beyond what the Indians' imaginations could produce, created absolutely paralyzing terror in many of them. Eventually the Ohlone would accept these beasts and come to believe that as they were children of the coyote, the Spanish were children of the mule.

Once the Spanish proved to be outwardly friendly, curiosity about the things that had frightened the Indians took over, and then the work of the missionaries began.

The padres, of course, were not interested in enslaving or destroying these simple people but wanted to save their souls by bringing Christianity to them. In fact the official position of the Spanish government was that once the Indians' lands were declared part of the Spanish Empire, the monarchy would regard them as full subjects with the rights and protections accorded everyone with that status.

The plan of the padres and the Spanish government was to bring the Indians into the missions for 10 years only. After their conversion to Christianity, the missions would become parish churches with Indian priests. The lands of the missions would then be divided, and the Indians could begin lives as Catholic farmers in quasi-utopian Christian communities.

Despite these good intentions, the new life for the Ohlone, as for remained very low. Women often induced abortions rather than bear mission children. This somewhat explains the incredible decline in the population of the Ohlone. The real nightmare, though, was disease. In the crowded environment of the missions, viruses brought with the Europeans were disseminated rapidly among the Indians, who had no immunity to the new sicknesses. Mumps, smallpox, influenza, and venereal diseases spread like wildfire. The pestilences sometimes killed up to 30 percent

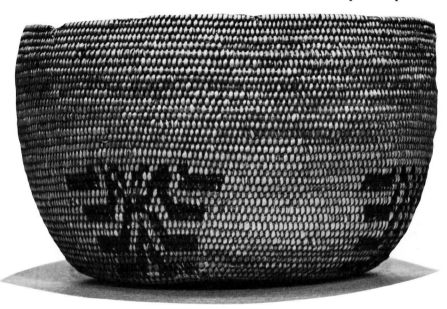

Above: *The baskets made by the Ohlone Indians were highly functional, but also an expression of creativity. Photo by Tanaka. Courtesy, San Mateo County Historical Association Archives*

Left: *The Ohlone fished the waters of San Francisco Bay in canoe-like vessels made from the reeds which grew along the water's edge. Courtesy, San Mateo County Historical Association Archives and The Bancroft Library*

most of the California Indians, was a harshly devastating one. After they accepted Christianity and were taken in at the missions, the men and women were forced to do hard work. The men tilled the soil. Women spun cloth. Promiscuity and other vices were severely and sometimes brutally punished. Under these conditions the birthrate of the Indians in a mission in one year.

After 10 years of mission life, the Ohlone were far from ready to lead their own lives as good Christians and full subjects of the Spanish throne. Instead, the Ohlone had been transformed into a weakened and dispirited people totally dependent upon the mission fathers for leadership. Under these circumstances, many of the monks became frustrated with their failure to mold the Indians to reflect their own dreams. Increased religious worship, hard work, and use of the whip often resulted.

Outside observers were frequently appalled over the condition of the Ohlone in the missions. Louis Choris wrote, "I have never seen one laugh." Otto von Kotzebue described their complete demoralization, saying the Ohlone had "their eyes . . . constantly fixed upon the ground."

Still, after its establishment in 1776, the Indians of the peninsula flocked to the padres at the Mission San Francisco de Asis, or Mission Dolores, as it is more commonly known.

It is difficult to explain completely why the Indians allowed themselves to become so captivated by the Spanish. However, it seems likely that the superior technologies of the Europeans must have mystified the Ohlone. Christianity and Christian music were attractive. The availability of different foods influenced some. Certainly, at least a few Indians were forced at gunpoint into the mission fold.

It is also possible that the Indians were awed by the Spaniards' ability to deal with the most frightening, brutal, and unconquerable enemy in their lives—the grizzly bear. This fearsome animal existed in great numbers on the peninsula and throughout California. Our local native people infrequently initiated quarrels with this beast, which they regarded as the devil himself. In fact, it might be said that the Ohlone were not on the top of the food chain, since where this huge killer roamed, the Ohlone made themselves scarce. When an encounter did occur, the Indians generally were on the losing end of any conflict. When they lived, their disfiguring wounds were a constant reminder to their tribelets of this terrifying element within their environment. When the Spanish arrived they often remarked upon what Padre Pedro Font referred to as the "many horrible examples" of grizzly bear attacks. Undoubtedly, when the Spanish demonstrated their ability to kill the beast with seemingly magical weaponry, it spawned gratitude and admiration among the original residents of the peninsula.

Once taken in by the Church, despite their unhappiness, the Ohlone generally displayed little willingness to resist the ways of the Spanish and the ultimate destruction of their culture and their very lives. However, there is some evidence that some Ohlone defied the Spanish. Some Indians ran away. The problem became so acute that the padres established what was called the "pasear," or walkabout. This allowed Indians to break the monotony of mission life once or twice a year by vacationing in or near their original homes, where they could collect their favorite foods and remember the old ways.

In 1789 a Salson called Charquin became the first of the runaways to show open resistance to the Spanish by raiding their fields and flocks. In 1794 he was captured and exiled. Another runaway Indian gained a great deal of notoriety as he roamed from Los Angeles to Marin County. Pomponio, after whom the creek and beach on the San Mateo County coast were named, for a time raided from a hideout along the peninsula's skyline. He was captured in 1823 in Marin County and executed in Monterey. After the mission days, some natives continued to disobey the laws and were often referred to as "horse-thief Indians." These individuals were the exceptions. By and large the Indians accepted the ways of the Spanish, and their fate. They did so because of their own beliefs.

The Ohlone were deeply fatalistic. They felt that they could do no better as a people than to hold on to the old ways. Their religious traditions told them that each passing generation was a little farther removed from the time of creation, and thus a bit less powerful and less able to function within their environment. A belief prevailed that indeed predicted an end to the ways of the past and destruction of the world as they knew it.

Their whole culture was therefore ill-suited for transition. The greatest successes that one could attain in life were not those that proved great innovative skills. One did not seek to rebel against, surpass, or improve upon the ways of the elders. Instead, the best one could do was to learn, remember, and pass on the habits of the past in a world which, before the Spanish, had not changed in centuries.

Finally, although the Ohlone were entrenched in the past, they had no history. According to their customs, a person's experiences, revelations, and thoughts died with him. It was forbidden to bring up the names of the dead. Therefore there was no record in the Ohlone's oral tradition of individuals who had come before and had either made changes that improved conditions or mastered unexpected situations. In the absence of knowledge of any such accomplishments in the past, innovation and progress were not viewed as possibilities for the future.

By 1832 the Ohlone population, which had been estimated to be about 10,000 in 1770, had shriveled to 2,000. In order to keep the work forces at the missions at adequate levels, Indians had long before been brought in from other parts of California.

After the Mexican Revolution, the missions were secularized —that is, their vast holdings were turned over to the state. As part of this process, the Indians of the peninsula were declared free to join any one of four mission communities, where they could establish lives for themselves. The communities were on lands desired by Spanish Californians, however, and Mexican land grantees sometimes forced the Indians off the properties.

In 1839 the entire community of Indians who had once belonged to the San Francisco Mission was moved to the San Mateo area, where an important mission outpost (discussed further in Chapter 2) had been established some years before. Here they remained for a number of years, cultivating individual plots inside a fenced field.

After the Bear Flag Revolt in 1846, the land, then known as Rancho San Mateo, ended up in the possession of an American merchant, W.D.M. Howard. He allowed the Indians to remain for some years. According to the California State Census, as many as 73 were still living there in 1852. Evidently their existence was not a cheerful one. One observer described them "as terrible beggers for potatoes and whiskey."

In 1852 Howard prepared for the visit of Sir Henry Vere Huntley, a famous English businessman. Various costly improvements were made to the rancho. El Camino Real near his place was fenced and graded. A farmhouse was constructed on top of an old Indian shell mound, and a mansion was constructed near the ruins of the old mission outpost. According to historian Alan K. Brown, the Indians at this time were "removed."

This drawing of an Indian ritual dance at Mission San Francisco evokes a lively picture of Indian life, in contrast to written descriptions that characterize the Ohlone as dispirited under mission rule. It is conceivable that European eyes viewed the situation inaccurately, possibly mistaking the natives' indifference for submission. Courtesy, Bancroft Library

THE ARRIVAL OF THE SPANISH

THE EXPLORERS

As early as 1522, the year after their conquest of the Aztecs, the Spanish became interested in the lands north of Mexico. Tales of magnificent wealth intrigued Hernando Cortes. Indian legends of seven cities and El Dorado, mixed with medieval myths of an island of Amazons, encouraged him to consider that the success he had achieved in Mexico could be repeated. Unfortunately for Cortes the few early expeditions launched were ill conceived and therefore failed. Finally, in the 1540s, Spain undertook two significant steps toward investigating much of what we know today as the western portion of the United States. On land, Francisco Vasquez de Coronado, in command of a

Facing page: *This drawing of a combination rodeo / cattle-branding event at an early California mission was probably made in the early nineteenth century. At that time the population of San Mateo County numbered far less than 1,000, and most of the cleared land was used for agriculture or cattle raising. Courtesy, San Mateo County Historical Association Archives*

The typical garb of the Spanish foot soldier was made of heavy homespun fabric, augmented with leather. Courtesy, San Mateo County Historical Association Archives

large and well-equipped party, explored the territory as far north as western Kansas. By sea, Juan Rodriguez Cabrillo sighted California and sailed as far as the Oregon border. Instead of returning with wealth and reports of advanced civilizations, these explorers revealed that no riches were to be found to the north and no great cities existed. All that was there was a rather harsh environment and hostile Indians.

For 60 years the Spanish did not make another major attempt to explore the region now known as California. In 1602 Sebastian Vizcaino, using his own capital, finally launched a voyage of exploration designed to chart the California coast. Vizcaino did so with the understanding that his reward for this task would be command of the next Manila treasure ship—a highly lucrative assignment. During his voyage he renamed much of the coast, and, upon his return, he said Monterey Bay was a fine protected port suitable for a Spanish settlement. Perhaps Vizcaino made this pronouncement feeling that a favorable report would help to ensure the reward he hoped for. Unfortunately for Vizcaino, the Spanish authorities in New Spain distrusted him. The reward of the Manila galleon was revoked, and Vizcaino's mapmaker, Martinez Palacios, was hanged for forgery.

Another 167 years passed before the Spanish felt it was again worthwhile to expend their limited resources on this isolated part of the world. In 1769, the Spanish became convinced that they must establish settlements in California or lose their claim to it. Because their naval power had diminished so greatly and that of their enemies, the English, had grown so powerfully, they determined that an overland expedition was desirable. Blazing a trail to the great natural harbor at Monterey (as it had been described by Vizcaino) became the goal for further explorations. A system of missions was planned, which would link Monterey with the rest of the Spanish empire. The problem of Spain's lack of laborers in the area would be solved by enlisting the local Indians, who would be made Spanish in religion, language, and through gradual intermixture of blood.

This renewed interest in California was sparked by Jose Galvez, who four years before had been appointed Visitor General of New Spain. For political reasons he wanted to give his sphere of influence the look of expansion and not decay. He justified the need for the California adventure through reports of Russian, Dutch, and English interest in the region.

Galvez called upon Captain Gaspar de Portola to lead the expedition. Portola had only months to prove himself a capable administrator by engineering the extremely difficult and personally disagreeable task of expelling the Jesuits from Baja California. This made room for the politically favored Franciscans, under Father Junipero Serra, who were to establish the missions in Upper California.

Portola was born in Catalon in 1717 to an aristocratic family. Since he had no chance as a second son to take over his family's affairs and no interest in a career in law or within the Church, he became a soldier. He entered the military at the age of 17 and was involved in numerous campaigns. Advancement was slow in coming. He spent eight years as an ensign and more than 25 years as a lieutenant before being promoted in 1768 to captain. His new orders were to report to New Spain and help lead the "Army of America," a task widely regarded as one of the worst possible assignments in the Spanish Army.

As Portola was receiving his orders from Galvez, he could not have been comforted by the fact that his superior was undergoing deep emotional strain. In fact, almost in the same manner that Galvez commanded Portola to explore California, he ordered 600 Guatemalan apes rounded up and put in uniform for action in putting down an Indian uprising in Sonora, Mexico.

Despite all doubts, like the good soldier he was, Portola followed his orders. Contact with Father Serra was established, and it was agreed that the expedition would be supported financially by the Baja missions. The overland party consisted of a number of neophytes (taken along to act as interpreters and examples for the Indians they would meet), a few dozen soldiers, blacksmiths, cooks, carpenters, one engineer, and one doctor. Three ships, the *San Carlos, San Antonio,* and *San Jose,* were to parallel the route of the land party, anchor at designated locations to come ashore and offer supplies to the weary marchers.

The land party set off on January 9, 1769, for the first rendezvous point—San Diego. The *San Antonio* reached this destination first, after 54 days. Inaccurate charts drawn from information presented by the Vizcaino expedition had San Diego too far to the north, and the ship had to double back. The *San Carlos* arrived three weeks later with a scurvy-ridden crew. Meanwhile, the land expedition reached San Diego with only about half its original complement of 300 people. Dozens who did reach the place were sick, and, at this point, the party's doctor went insane.

The *San Antonio* was sent back to Mexico for more supplies, and Portola, as ordered, set out for Monterey. He took with him most of the healthy soldiers and Father Serra's capable assistant, Juan Crespi. Serra remained in San Diego to care for the sick and to establish California's first mission.

Portola's route largely followed today's Highway 101. His plan called for meeting the *San Jose* at Monterey and then exploring the harbor. The *San Jose,* however, was

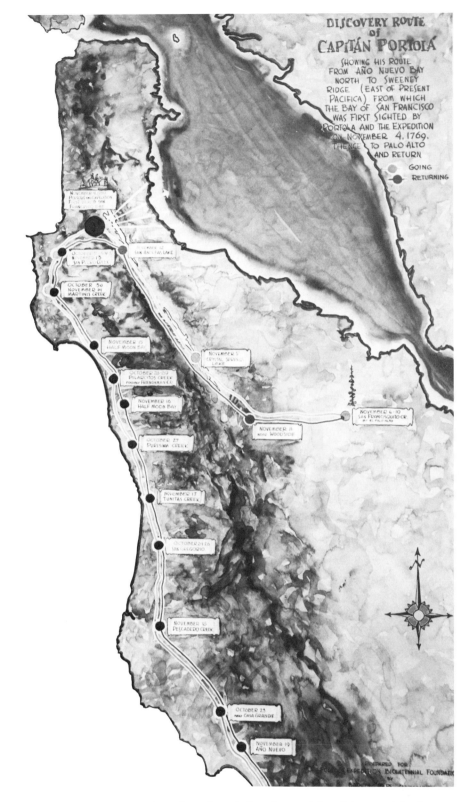

Upon reaching San Mateo County's southern tip, Portola traveled north to present-day Sweeney Ridge in Pacifica, where he sighted San Francisco Bay. An attempt to travel around the bay by land was abandoned at San Francisquito Creek (in present-day Palo Alto) and the expedition returned to San Diego. Map prepared by Expedition Bicentennial Foundation. Courtesy, San Mateo County Historical Association Archives

This is a recent view of the Sanchez Adobe, a historic site owned by the County of San Mateo and operated by the San Mateo County Historical Association. Located on Linde Mar Boulevard in Pacifica, the adobe is open to visitors several days a week. The grounds include reconstructions of several Indian huts which existed there when the land was a mission outpost. Courtesy, San Mateo County Historical Archives

never heard from again after it left Mexico, and when Portola reached Monterey, he could not believe that this was the great natural harbor that Vizcaino had described. The party therefore continued northward.

Late in October, as the rainy season began, Portola entered what is known today as San Mateo County. On the last day of the month, camp was made at Point San Pedro. Here the explorers understood some Indians to say that a ship was anchored to the north. The party hoped that the rendezvous with the *San Jose* might now materialize. Scouts climbed up the hills to the east in order to get a better view, and, from what today is called Sweeney Ridge in Pacifica, beheld the San Francisco Bay for the first time.

Unfortunately Portola's men could not see the Golden Gate from their position. Intervening hills prevented them from discovering how close they were to the entrance of one of the world's greatest estuaries. An attempt was made to march around the bay by going as far south as Palo Alto, but this was

given up on November 11, and the party decided to turn back. Portola wrote that he had "found nothing." In great despair the expedition began its march south. After subsisting on 12 of their mules, the party reached San Diego on January 24, 1770.

While Portola's reports were negative about the new lands they had seen, Father Crespi's opinions were positive. Crespi also recognized the significance of the discovery of the great body of water. He convinced Galvez that more exploration and support were appropriate.

In 1770 Galvez sent Portola and Serra north again: Serra by sea and Portola overland. Together they founded Monterey. Father Serra made the new mission his headquarters. Meanwhile Portola retired, but his replacement, Lieutenant Pedro Fages, led a small party northward. In November this party finally sighted the Golden Gate from the East Bay, thereby proving the importance of Portola's earlier discovery and the strategic significance of the peninsula for Spain as it tried to hold on to California.

THE MISSIONARIES

Crespi's description of the bay and Fages' discovery of its entrance gave the Spanish enough information to determine that their presence on the peninsula was essential to their mastery of California. From the peninsula they could control access to the greatest estuary in the region.

The Spanish were concerned about maintaining their lines of supply and communication on land because of English naval superiority. In order to strengthen the overland network of support and bring fresh settlers to establish a mission and presidio at the tip of the peninsula, Captain Juan Bautista de Anza was called on to open a land route from Sonora, Mexico, to Monterey and the future San Francisco Mission.

De Anza successfully blazed the trail in 1775 and, in less than one year, began a second expedition from Sonora—this one with soldiers and their families—for the specific purpose of creating the new mission and presidio. After some delays in Monterey, Lieutenant Jose Moraga and Friar Francisco Palou led the pioneers and 300 head of cattle to the tip of the peninsula.

The first mission building was made of wood and was completed on October 9, 1776. The structure now standing, which is commonly referred to as Mission Dolores, was constructed between 1788 and 1791. The Mission San Francisco de Asis' territory extended south all the way to San Francisquito Creek, the present boundary between San Mateo and Santa Clara counties.

Cattle were the most important resource brought by the Spanish. The meat kept the early settlement fed, while hides were used for shelter, beds, saddles, ropes, thongs, and binding materials.

The Fathers made progress early on with a tribelet of Indians living close to the mission. Another band of Ohlone, probably Salson from further south on the peninsula, attacked this group, however, fearing an alliance between them and the Spanish. This delayed activities for a while, but relations were finally renewed in March 1777. On June 24 the first baptism occurred. During the next dozen years, many chiefs and whole tribelets from the peninsula joined the Church. By 1793 virtually all the Ohlone living in the region under the care of the Mission San Francisco de Asis were Christians.

In an organized way and for very practical reasons, the Spanish moved the Indians back down the peninsula after their conversion. The Presidio of San Francisco had been established near the northern tip of the peninsula for sound strategic purposes, and the mission was built close by for its own security. Besides protection, however, the mission needed other things in order to be successful. Such neces-

Francisco de Haro was alcalde *of the village of Yerba Buena (now San Francisco) and son-in-law of Jose Sanchez. He assisted his father-in-law in measuring the boundaries of Rancho Buri Buri using methods which, by present-day standards, would be judged considerably less than accurate. Courtesy, San Mateo County Historical Association Archives*

sities included readily available wood and water, plenty of grazing land, good soil, and an adequate climate for growing crops. After all, the mission had hundreds of neophytes in training, and they had to be fed. These essentials did not exist at the northern end of the pen-

insula. Therefore outposts were established to the south in today's San Mateo County.

Between 1785 and 1786 the first such hospice was created in the San Pedro Valley (today's Linda Mar area in Pacifica). The soil here proved fertile and success seemed inevitable. In fact the neophytes, under the guidance of the padres, built 2,760 yards of fencing and planted pear trees, peach trees, grape vines, 36 acres of wheat, and nine acres of corn. Unfortunately, in 1791 communicable diseases (discussed in Chapter 1) had a disastrous effect on this thriving enterprise, and it was abandoned.

Perhaps four or five other outposts were established down the peninsula, but none could compare in food production with the San Mateo hospice, which was initiated in 1793 (at what is roughly Baywood Avenue and El Camino Real today). At one time this hospice's neophytes numbered over 1,000, under the supervision of two lone padres. Even after the ravaging epidemics of the 1790s, San Mateo was noted for maintaining 10,000 head of sheep, 10,000 head of cattle, and hundreds of horses and mules.

The herds of the outposts that supported the San Francisco Mission grazed as far south as Tunitas Creek along the coast and San Francisquito Creek on the bayside. In 1812, the peak year for the wheat harvest, some 11,098 bushels were yielded. Without a doubt, the productive work of the hospices on the peninsula was responsible for keeping the mission in San Francisco operational. They deserved much of the credit for its success.

THE RANCHEROS
In 1821 Mexico gained its indepen-

Life on the early California ranchos was difficult, and entertainment was often less than refined. Here a crowd looks on for its amusement as a bull and bear fight. Courtesy, San Mateo County Historical Association Archives

dence from Spain. For individuals living in the San Francisco Mission community, the greatest implication of this event was the promise of secularization of mission lands by the new government. It took 10 years, but in 1831 the San Francisco Mission properties were taken over by the state. The plan was for the mission to function as a parish church, enabling the lands it once held to be divided up and granted to individuals for use as privately owned ranchos.

The rather loosely observed rules of the land grants stated that the real estate could not be sold and that each grantee should plant trees and construct a house (thus demonstrating an interest in improving the property and making it productive). Before the Mexican American War, some 500 land grants were issued in California. Some grants were as large as 100,000 acres. The 17 given within the present borders of San Mateo County were comparatively small due to the fact that the quality of the land was high, and there was more demand for it.

Grantees were many times influential soldiers under the old Spanish regime. A good example was Jose Antonio Sanchez. He and his parents had come to California with the Anza expedition of 1776. Following in his father's footsteps, he became a soldier and was assigned to the San Francisco Presidio in 1791. Here he rose in rank from private to lieutenant. In anticipation of secularization, Sanchez took possession of a 15,000-acre parcel, which had once been used as grazing lands for the Spanish garrison, known as Rancho Buri Buri. In 1835 it legally became his. Sanchez's property included much of

today's northern Burlingame, Millbrae, San Bruno, South San Franciso, and southern Mount San Bruno.

The society of the rancho period was based on cattle. The California herds were the first great ones of the West. The Spanish longhorn was well suited for grazing on the grasses of the range. Sanchez engaged in agricultural pursuits, but most rancho owners did not. Farming was deemed beneath their dignity, while cattle raising was judged to be gentlemanly. Life for the rancheros could be easy and relatively carefree. Cattle were identified by brands and allowed to roam unfettered.

Besides secularization, the greatest change to this part of the world brought about by the Mexican Revolution was the introduction of free trade. For the first time ships from around the world were allowed to trade in California ports. Yankee sailing ships became a frequent sight, as all sorts of manufactured goods were traded for the two great exports, hides and tallow. Both, of course, derived from the cattle.

The rancheros were rich in land and cattle, but essentially lived a cash-poor existence. In fact, money seldom changed hands and was used more as a measure of who owed what to whom. The rancheros were often in debt for years after purchasing manufactured goods, but were regarded as good risks because they were men of honor.

Indians, once part of the mission's outpost system, were many times kept as laborers on the ranchos in a feudal-type arrangement. A few of the most favored were allowed to become vaqueros, but only with special permission was a

Native American allowed on horseback. Indians with riding abilities who turned against the rancho owners became fearsome enemies. Those with mixed blood frequently did become vaqueros. These incredibly skilled, original cowboys of the West participated in all the traditional open-range activities (round ups, rodeos, etc.) associated with cattle raising.

Despite the change from Spanish to Mexican rule, California stayed a remote place, cut off from the rest of Mexico's territories by mountains to the east and desert and unfriendly Indians to the south. The population remained sparse. The number of people within today's San Mateo County, including Indians, probably was not more than 500 as late as 1845.

Under these primitive conditions, the rancheros of the peninsula were left pretty much to govern their own affairs. For example, when it came time to measure Jose Sanchez's land grant, Sanchez's son-in-law, Francisco de Haro (who happened to be alcalde of the village of Yerba Buena, later known as San Francisco), was asked to preside over the enterprise. De Haro assembled a group of men at Point San Bruno to begin the activity. The procedure for surveying consisted of having two mounted men take turns riding past one another stretching a rawhide lariat measuring one vera (about 50 yards) between them. When the group approached Mount San Bruno, it was determined that climbing it would be more trouble than it was worth, and so an estimate of its dimensions was made. In this manner the entire 25-mile border of the rancho, containing four square leagues (or 15,000 acres) of property, were covered in one day. Then, according to the document awarding Sanchez the grant, "Said citizen Jose Sanchez pulled up grass and stones from the ground and threw them to the four winds as a sign of his legal possession."

Sanchez became the most prosperous and influential rancho owner on the peninsula. He built his home on the El Camino Real, where Millbrae and Burlingame meet today. On a nearby slough he constructed an embarcadero, or boat landing, for his shipments of hides and tallow. His herd of cattle was initially counted at 2,000, and he had 250 horses. These numbers were known to have multiplied greatly.

Sanchez's family also successfully pursued properties down the peninsula. His son, Francisco, acquired the 8,926-acre San Pedro Rancho, which included much of present-day Pacifica. In 1839 the younger Sanchez built a temporary dwelling in the San Pedro Valley, shortly before receiving title. Between 1842 and 1846 he constructed an adobe house on the site of the old mission outpost. This structure still stands on Linda Mar Boulevard. Like his father, Francisco was a leader of men. At age 32 he was chosen captain of the civic militia, and in 1842, at age 37, he was made alcalde of Yerba Buena.

Other Sanchez family members who acquired land grants on the peninsula included Jose's son-in-law, de Haro, who received Rancho Laguna de la Merced in today's Daly City area, and Jose's grandson, Domingo Feliz, who was given a rancho that bore his own last name in today's watershed region.

While the Sanchezes by and large lived and worked on their ranchos, others down the peninsula did not. For example, the Rancho de Las Pulgas was awarded to the widow of former Presidio Commander and Governor of California Luis Arguello in 1835. The Arguello family only lived there for a while, even though it was the largest grant on the peninsula (35,250 acres). This rancho stretched from current downtown San Mateo to San Francisquito Creek.

With the advent of the Bear Flag Revolt and the Mexican American War, some absentee owners went to live at their ranchos to avoid the turmoil. The Vasquez family, who were from the San Francisco community, moved to their land grant on the coast side of the peninsula, which was isolated and safe from the hostilities. They built their home a little north of Pilarcitos Creek. The Miramontes family, who owned the rancho south of the creek, constructed their family adobe only yards away on their side of the rivulet. A small village of sorts resulted, which the residents called San Benito. Over the hill, the Americans called it Spanishtown, in reference to its role as a sanctuary for Spanish speaking people. It later became known as Half Moon Bay.

Don Luis Antonio Gonzaga Tranquillino Arguello, first native-born governor of California, and his wife, Donna Maria Angela Berryesa de Arguello, are pictured. Rancho de las Pulgas, comprising much of mid- and south San Mateo County, was awarded to the Arguello family. Courtesy, San Mateo County Historical Association Archives

THE AMERICAN PERIOD BEGINS

EARLY DEVELOPMENT

Even before the United States took control of California in 1847, Americans were conspicuous on the peninsula. In fact Jacob Leese, who became a Mexican citizen, was granted the 9,500-acre Rancho Guadalupe La Visitacion Y Rodeo Viejo in 1841 (it consisted of today's Brisbane and the northern half of Mount San Bruno). W.D.M. Howard with Henry Mellus purchased the Rancho San Mateo (much of today's San Mateo, Burlingame, and Hillsborough) in 1846.

However, the earliest and most numerous group of Americans resided in the redwood country in the area of Woodside and Kings Mountain. Beginning in the early 1830s, Americans and Europeans from a variety of nations managed

Facing page: *This photo was probably taken at the Redwood City boat landing by late nineteenth century photographer James Van Court. The lumber was stacked and rafted north on the bay with the tide; later, lumber barges were used. Courtesy, San Mateo County Historical Association Archives*

to jump ship at Yerba Buena and find their way to the hill country, where they became sawyers.

This group of men found themselves continually at odds with Mexican officials for tax dodging and the construction of stills. Of more concern to the sawyers than the revenuers, however, were the ferocious grizzly bears that continued to prowl the peninsula. It has been estimated that the grizzly bear population of California doubled during the rancho period, since the grizzlies thrived on the cattle of the open range, and there is plenty of evidence to suggest that the beasts were numerous on the peninsula.

Two American sawyers, Bill Smith and George Ferguson, had a bear pass through their camp one night in 1835. The next day they constructed a trap by digging a pit. That night a bear was caught, and they tried to crush it to death with a

Charles Brown, originally from New York, arrived in California in 1833. He purchased 2,000 acres of San Mateo land and created the county's first sawmill in 1849. Brown married the daughter of Antonio Garcia of San Jose. Courtesy, San Mateo County Historical Association Archives

log. After this failed and the bear escaped, Smith went to Yerba Buena and purchased an old musket. The two men killed a steer when Smith returned and used it for bait. They then shot three bears in the hours between sunset and early morning.

Perhaps the most celebrated grizzly bear incident of the hill country occurred a few years later. A man named Ryder stopped for a drink of water at the bottom of one of the local ravines. He lost half his ear when a great female grizzly attacked him. Thereafter he was called "Grizzly Ryder," and the ravine became known as "Bear Gulch."

After the Bear Flag Revolt, the sawyers noted little increase in the demand for lumber. This changed in 1849, however, with the discovery of gold in the foothills of the Sierras and the rapid growth of San Francisco. During the 1850s San Francisco frequently suffered from disastrous fires. Each time, lumber from the southern San Mateo County hill country helped to make new construction possible.

Charles Brown created the first sawmill in 1849. Brown owned the 2,800-acre Mountain Home Ranch, which stretched between the Alambique and Bear gulches. Willard Whipple bought out Brown soon after operations began.

In 1852 the firm of Baker and Burnham initiated the first really large mill works, again in the vicinity of Bear Gulch. Their Gang Mill possessed 26 upright saws, two edgers, and a planer run off of two engines powered by three boilers.

By 1853 there were 14 mills active in the Kings Mountain area. One of the most successful was operated by a Frenchman named

Eugene Froment. He placed his mill between the headwaters of the Tunitas and Purissima canyons. Around his mill sprang up a small village called Grabtown. It probably got its name because the company owned all the land and the small workers' shacks. Those needing shelter literally grabbed up the meager dwellings when they became vacant. Nothing remains of Grabtown. It burned to the ground before the turn of the century.

At the height of the lumber business, Henry King and his wife came to the mountain area that eventually took their name. They built a shack on land belonging partly to the Greer family, partly to businessmen George R. Borden and Rufus H. Hatch, and partly to the government. They operated a saloon at first and later built a boardinghouse alongside of it. The location of the structures, which were quite popular into the present century, was at the junction of Skyline Boulevard and Woodside Road.

With the lumber industry booming, two small ports developed almost simultaneously to handle the transport of lumber to San Francisco.

In 1849 Isaiah C. Woods established docking facilities at Ravenswood (today's East Palo Alto). This was probably the best location along the South County's bayline to find good anchorage. Nearby were potentially productive agricultural lands and the lumbering areas. Ravenswood failed, however, perhaps due to the questionable business dealings of its founder (Woods was eventually "run out of town") and competition from the other port to the north.

M.A. Parkhurst and Dr. R.O. Tripp also recognized the potential for the lumber industry in the south county, and, with financial backing from interests in San Francisco, they established a landing in today's Redwood City area. Using oxen for power, they dragged their hand-squared timbers and round logs to a point along the slough that is now behind the buildings on the northwest corner of Broadway and Main streets. Here the lumber was tied together to form rafts. When the tide went out, the wood was floated out to the bay and then escorted by sailing craft to San Francisco. As squatters moved in around the embarcadero, an infant town was born.

Woodside was more of a community, at least in terms of population, during the 1850s. For instance, in 1859, while there were 85 pupils in the Redwood City School District, there were close to 200 in the two Woodside area districts. In addition, the county's first library association was founded in Woodside.

The center of this hill-country community was the Woodside Store, which stands today at the intersection of Tripp and King's Mountain roads. It was founded by the energetic duo of Parkhurst and Tripp. Besides serving as an emporium stocking every imaginable type of commodity, the place functioned as the post office and a community meeting place. One could even have a tooth pulled there. For some years Dr. Tripp was the only dentist in the county.

Elsewhere in the county other Americans established themselves. In the north, Charles Lux bought 1,500 acres of Rancho Buri Buri property, the site of present-day South San Francisco. Here he built a home and, after forming his famous partnership with Henry

Steam-powered planing devices were used in early San Mateo lumbering. The workers standing atop a fallen tree at the right indicate the size of the virgin redwoods in the county. San Mateo County lumber provided much of the building material for early San Francisco. Courtesy, San Mateo County Historical Association Archives

Workers at the Virginia Mill in Purissima Canyon posed for this photo, circa 1906, after Alvin Hatch purchased the mill. Fred Wend, mill foreman, is standing third from the left. Herman Gisler, the woodsman who felled the trees and brought them to the mill, is seated on a log, second from the right. The mill's Chinese cook is fifth from the right in the back row. Courtesy, San Mateo County Historical Association Archives

Miller, made the place an assembly point for their vast cattle empire. Also in the north county, a group of 21 Americans, many of whom were young veterans of the Mexican American War, settled on property northwest of Rancho Buri Buri in order to start small farms.

On the coast side, James Johnston obtained 1,162 acres of land south of Spanishtown from Candelario Miramontes for $14,000. Johnston, a former Indian fighter from Ohio, had been one of the lucky Forty-Niners who actually struck it rich. With his fortune he bought part ownership in one of San Francisco's famous gambling houses, the El Dorado Saloon. The enterprise put him in contact with many of the old Mexican families, enabling him to meet and marry Petra de Jara in 1852. Johnston became acquainted with Miramontes through the marriage.

When Johnston and his wife went to live on Miramontes' former property, they determined it would

become a dairy ranch. Johnston sent for his brothers, William, Thomas, and John, who drove a dairy herd all the way from Ohio to the coast side of San Mateo. It is reported that of all the hardships faced on the journey, the most difficult part of the adventure was guiding the herd over the coastal hills on the peninsula, where adequate roads still did not exist.

In the mid-county area, W.D.M. Howard bought out his partner's share of Rancho San Mateo and built the county's first mansion, known as El Cerrito. Here too, Nicholas de Peyster established the county's first roadhouse. De Peyster moved into the old mission hospice building and created a store and public house. Although told repeatedly to get off the property, which was part of Rancho San Mateo, de Peyster stayed there until 1851, when he bought 75 acres of Pulgas land across San Mateo Creek. He then built a hotel known as the San Mateo or Halfway

While felling one of the giant trees which gave Redwood City its name, these loggers paused for a photograph. The saws in the foreground indicate the direction in which the tree was cut to fall. The photo was probably taken in the latter part of the nineteenth century. Courtesy, San Mateo County Historical Association Archives

House, which became an important stagecoach stop. Eventually roadhouses, some much more primitive than de Peyster's, lined the El Camino Real, mile after mile, from San Francisco to San Jose. The San Mateo establishment was known as the Halfway House because of its location midway between the two cities.

During the 10-year period from 1849 to 1859, these Americans and many others radically changed the peninsula. The open range rapidly gave way to clusters of farms that stretched from one end of the county to the other—on the bay side, on the coast side, and down the center of the peninsula, now filled with manmade lakes. In 1860 San Mateo County marketed 200,000 pounds of butter, 23,000 pounds of cheese, 165,000 bushels of wheat, 100,000 bushels of oats, and 2,882 barrels of beans, along

Founded by Parkhurst and Tripp in 1851, the Woodside Store continued to operate until 1909. In 1932 the building was declared a state landmark. Purchased by the county of San Mateo in 1940, the building has recently undergone extensive restoration, including internal reconstruction. The Woodside Store is open to the public. Courtesy, San Mateo County Historical Association Archives

with quantities of corn, rice, wool, mutton, beef, and pork.

In order to support this farming industry, small towns developed. On the bay side, Redwood City had 500 residents by 1860 and became, in 1867, the first town in the county to incorporate. On the coast side, Half Moon Bay rivaled Redwood City in size, while Purissima and Pescadero also attracted growing numbers of people.

The 1860 Census indicates that the total population of the county was more than 5,300, approximately 1,000 percent more than in 1849. That harbinger of nineteenth-century progress, the railroad, was already planned, and by the beginning of 1864 a track was laid and in operation connecting San Francisco and San Jose.

A LEGACY OF CORRUPTION

When California became a state in 1850, most of what we now consider San Mateo County became part of San Francisco County. This division followed the old mission boundaries.

San Francisco itself was a growing, pulsating city. By 1856 it had a population of 50,000 and was the most important urban community on the Pacific Slope of North America. South of the city, the peninsula was a rural farm and lumbering belt. The political interests of those living in today's San Mateo County were represented in San Francisco by Dr. Tripp of Woodside, who served as a county supervisor.

As early as 1855, residents south of the city tried to get a new county formed, which was to be called Raymundo. They believed that the interests of the city were very different from their own and that San Francisco was too far away to be county seat. In 1856 this group of citizens found some unexpected supporters in a roundabout way.

Aided by former governor John McDougal, a resident of Belmont, unscrupulous politicos and others attempted to gain control of San Mateo County through rigged election results. Their efforts were unsuccessful, partially due to the investigation of election improprieties initiated by newly elected Judge Ben Fox of Redwood City. Courtesy, San Mateo County Historical Association Archives

State Assemblyman Horace Hawes introduced a bill to consolidate San Francisco's city and county governments, circa 1856. Because of a political compromise, the creation of San Mateo County from the southern portion of San Francisco County was appended to this bill. Corrupt San Francisco politicians, deprived of the opportunity to move from city to county government posts, sought control of the new county government in San Mateo. Courtesy, San Mateo County Historical Association Archives

Silhouetted against a stormy coastside sky, the New England saltbox architecture of the Johnston House contrasts sharply with the California coastal hills. After this photograph was taken, the Johnston House Foundation undertook restoration and renovation of the building. Exterior restoration is completed. The house is not open to the public, but may be seen from Highway 1 just south of the town of Half Moon Bay. Photo by Lloyd L. Reise. Courtesy, San Mateo County Historical Association Archives

In San Francisco a consolidation movement was afoot because having two governments (city and county) made it difficult to mount a reform campaign to eliminate corrupt politicians. It seemed that every time the rascals were routed out of one government, they found shelter in the other. Consequently State Assemblyman Horace Hawes introduced a bill in Sacramento to combine the two. However, the more lawless sector had many allies in the state capital, and a compromise resulted. According to contemporary observer Benjamin Lathrop, the new agreement forced Hawes "to make terms with the thieves by adding a clause to his act cutting off about 9/10 of the County of San Francisco, establishing what is now the County of San Mateo." Lathrop explained that this act was acceptable to the "gang" because it also called for organizing the new county government immediately, which would allow them the opportunity to seize control.

Thus, the reformers gained because the Consolidation Act merged San Francisco's county and city governments into one unit. It also forced some city officials to become bonded and fixed expenditures for five city departments.

The "roughs," on the other hand, were given a new county to be organized without delay. They could control San Mateo County without the interference of reformers from San Francisco, and they could run all their rackets from south of the county line while waiting in security for better times and the opportunity to return to San Francisco.

Who were these "thieves," as Lathrop labeled them? There actually existed two factions, according to California historian Herbert Howe Bancroft. He believed that corrupt politicians and criminals had joined forces to prey on society. Criminals stuffed ballot boxes and intimidated voters in order to elect their political friends, who in return did their best to get this lawless element excused from justice when they were caught for their crimes.

Most visible in the effort to control San Mateo County was Chris Lilly. He owned the Abbey House on the top of the hill at what is today the intersection of San Jose Avenue and Mission Street in Daly City. This came to be the operating center of the gang. The county line initially was drawn one mile south of this location, but it was later pulled north so that the Abbey House could be included in the new county.

An interesting cast of characters supported Lilly. William Mulligan, a prizefighter from New York, had a Tammany Hall background and performed some of the more infa-

Benjamin Lathrop, early San Mateo County supervisor, resided in Redwood City. His home has been preserved and is open to the public. Courtesy, San Mateo County Historical Association Archives

mous acts in the ensuing election. Also allied with Lilly was former California Lieutenant Governor John McDougal.

McDougal joined forces with this group in order to have Belmont, the location of his home, declared county seat. According to Bancroft, McDougal was a "gentlemanly drunkard, and a democratic politician of the order for which California was destined to become somewhat unpleasantly notorious." He had been superintendent of Ohio's state prison until 1846, when he became a captain in the war against Mexico. At the end of the hostilities, he came to California. Bancroft described him as "fine-looking," adhering to "the old style of ruffled shirt front, buff vest and pantaloons, and blue coat with brass buttons." Bancroft tells us "that there were two things of whom he stood in awe—God almighty and Mrs. McDougal—the latter always treated him with patient kindness, although often compelled to bring him home from a midnight debauch." Bancroft insists that, as lieutenant governor, "he was seldom fit for the discharge of his duties," yet "such was the influence of his natural genial and generous deportment, cultivated mind, and brilliant social talents, that only his political enemies, and not always those, could bring themselves to treat him with the contempt another man in his position would have received."

In "organizing" the new county, the plan of the gang was to have the elections before the local residents could catch on to what was happening. Therefore, although the Consolidation Act was not scheduled to go into effect until July, the election was scheduled for May. On voting day, Lilly's forces seized three of the county's 13 polling stations and ran the election booths. They stuffed the ballot boxes with votes for their candidates, using the names of hundreds of passengers recently arrived by ship, whose real identities would be untraceable.

Because of these methods 297 ballots were tallied at the Laguna Precinct in Crystal Springs Valley, which probably had not more than 25 eligible voters. At the Abbey House, where the precinct had less than 50 real voters, some 500 ballots were cast. In Belmont votes were compiled in the home of former Lieutenant Governor McDougal, and local observers were not allowed in to witness the count. Mulligan and his men gathered all the ballots, and tabulation began at the American Hotel in Redwood City, where the roughs conspicuously displayed their weapons and further intimidated the locals. They also denied election judges John Johnston of Half Moon Bay and Charles Clark of Colma the right to inspect the votes. The third judge, Dr. Tripp, recognized the election for what it was and refused to take any part in monitoring the corrupt affair.

The results were obviously favorable to Lilly and company. Out of a total population of 2,500, some 1,800 ballots were counted (in the days when women did not vote!). Lilly's bartender, Robert Gray, was elected county clerk. Mulligan's brother, Bernard, became sheriff. Other Lilly men assumed positions such as county attorney, assessor, and treasurer. The gang also won one of the three county supervisors' seats.

Thus a stranglehold was put on the infant county. Fortunately some honest men also won offices. Ben Fox of Redwood City became a judge and immediately initiated an investigation into the election. Johnston also won one of the supervisors' seats and Clark defeated Lilly's ally, James Casey, for the third supervisor's position.

Three days after the election, Casey became the focus of attention in the *San Francisco Bulletin,* a newspaper edited by James King of William. The *Bulletin* revealed that Casey had served time at Sing Sing, the New York state penitentiary. Because of this exposure, Casey visited King and threatened him in his office. An hour later Casey shot and killed King on the street.

This incident sparked the creation of the famous San Francisco Vigilance Committee of 1856. Casey was hanged, and most of the other members of the gang, including Lilly and William Mulligan, were forced to leave the state. New elections were then held for San Mateo County, and a more law-abiding government was established.

The implications for San Francisco and San Mateo County were far-reaching.

San Francisco had lost much. Soon San Franciscans would be forced to rely on San Mateo County for their water supply, for a place to bury their dead, and, later on, for an important airport. San Francisco's ability to expand in geographical size and tax base subsequently was limited to the very northern tip of the peninsula.

The implications also were great for San Mateo County. For decades it remained a sparsely settled rural region, slower growing than any other county in the Bay Area, primarily because of its proximity to San Francisco. Almost all development focused on the great metropolis to the north.

Still worse, as San Francisco's rural neighbor, San Mateo County continued for all these years to be known as a place where, if you could not "get away with it" in San Francisco, you could come down to the "country" and do it. Just as Lilly and Mulligan felt they could fix elections in San Mateo County, others were able to participate in a variety of activities there that were illegal in San Francisco. When California Chief Justice David S. Terry and Senator David C. Broderick decided to settle their differences in 1859 by dueling, they crossed the county line near Lake Merced and shot it out. In later years when dog racing, horse racing, and prizefighting became illegal in San Francisco, facilities were established in San Mateo County.

Alcohol-producing stills, present in the county since the 1830s, became extremely numerous during the 1920s. The amount of illegal activity during Prohibition was appalling. Nearly every large structure down along the coast served as a speakeasy at one time or another. Large criminal organizations had their "rum running" ships and boats make routine landings on San Mateo County beaches and then trucked hundreds of thousands of gallons of "hootch" from the isolated coves near the coast highway to the city.

After Prohibition ended in 1933 the county's reputation did not improve. In fact, right up to the early 1950s, San Mateo County was widely known as being the most corrupt or "wide open" county in California. This was the legacy of its creation in 1856.

4

REGIONAL HISTORIES

Until World War II the different sections of the county developed in ways that made them quite unique. Geography had much to do with this phenomenon.

For the north county, the great dominating factor was its proximity to San Francisco. For the mid-county area it was the readily accessible natural recreational assets. For the south county the presence of redwood trees in the nearby hills was crucial. The coast side's experience was affected by its physical isolation. The bay lands became valuable because of the rich environmental conditions of the great estuary of which they were a part. Finally, the valleys in the middle of the county were ideal for the creation of water reservoirs.

Facing page: *At the turn of the century, those who couldn't afford horse-drawn carriages used bicycles to get around San Mateo County. Paul Noisat's San Mateo Cyclery sold, rented, and repaired bicycles. Courtesy, San Mateo County Historical Association Archives*

John Donald Daly, who was a pioneer dairy rancher and builder in northern San Mateo County, gave Daly City its name. He is shown here in a late nineteenth century photograph. In 1906, following the San Francisco earthquake, Daly supplied homes for refugees from fire-torn San Francisco. Courtesy, Samuel C. Chandler History Collection, Daly City

NORTH COUNTY

During the nineteenth century much of what we know of today as Daly City and Colma was collectively referred to as Colma. In the 1850s and 1860s activity in the area clustered around a small trading center at the intersection of Mission Street and Old San Pedro Road. The place abounded with gambling and drinking houses. In addition one could find card and dice games in the grocery and dry goods stores. After San Mateo became a separate county in 1856, law enforcement was more of a rarity than it had been before, and the character of the community became almost legendary. Some said that Mission Street featured "the finest mile and a half of eating and drinking found anywhere in the country." Indeed, the saloons became well-known for special Sunday dinners. Competition was fierce as each tried to outdo the others. For the saloon patrons,

Northern San Mateo County became a staging area for boxing matches in the early part of the century. Matches featuring young boxers, like the ones who posed for this 1903 photograph, were favorite sporting events in the county, and drew spectators from San Francisco. Courtesy, San Mateo County Historical Association Archives

free lunches were routinely served, which consisted of cuts of meat, cheeses, and various breads. By 1890 the place had not changed much. Of the 20 businesses present, six were saloons. All the way up to the verge of Prohibition, in fact, drinking establishments dominated. In 1915, of the 49 businesses, 15 were saloons.

By the turn of the century, this Colma area had attracted a variety of activities that San Francisco had either outlawed or had no room for. For example, the north county's

proximity to San Francisco made it the logical location for the placement of dog tracks. One occupied the present site of Jefferson High School.

In 1903 James W. Coffroth built a boxing arena only 50 feet away from the county line. Many of the greatest contests of the era, including Jack Johnson bouts, took place there. Because of the arena's placement in San Mateo County, the San Francisco police had no jurisdiction. North county residents therefore were often recruited as "deputies" to keep order around the ring. These individuals evidently had plenty to do, as the excitement among the crowds often led to bloodier fights outside the ring than in it.

In addition to having a reputation for catering to the leisure-time activities of San Franciscans, the north county was also known as an agricultural and dairy ranch region. First Irish and then Italian farmers came to the area in great numbers. Once again proximity to the city gave farmers easy access to a substantial market. Between 1866 and 1877, the Irish faced a terrible decade of thicker than usual fogs and a potato blight. To an extent, they were succeeded by Italians, who successfully established truck gardening and flower growing. In 1853 J.G. Knowles established a dairy within today's Daly City. It was the first of many north county operations that produced milk products for sale in San Francisco.

Among the laborers at these early dairies was a boy named John D. Daly. He and his mother set out for California from the East during the Gold Rush, but his mother died while traversing the Isthmus of Panama. Daly then came to California alone. He worked for others until 1868, when he bought his own dairy with money he had saved. He specialized in milk and egg production for the San Francisco market. Daly's 250-acre ranch eventually

The renowned and the unknown share space in Colma's many cemeteries. This monument, marking the gravesite of Thomas Larkin, United States Consul to Mexican California prior to the annexation of California by the United States, is at Cypress Lawn. Other notables buried in Colma include James C. Flood, "Emperor" Norton, and Wyatt Earp. Courtesy, Samuel C. Chandler History Collection, Daly City

contained a ranch house and barns that were said to be among the largest structures in the north county. A dozen men were under his employ when the dairy was running at its peak at the turn of the century.

Because of San Francisco's shortage of real estate, the north county also became a place to bury the city's dead. The Roman Catholic Church consecrated Holy Cross, the first cemetery in the Colma area, in 1887. Many others followed. In 1888 the Jewish cemetery, Home of Peace, was established. Later the Italian, Chinese, Serbian, Japanese, and Greek communities created their own resting places. In 1892 Cypress Lawn began operations and was acclaimed one of the most beautiful, nonsectarian burial grounds in the United States.

The cemeteries became one of San Mateo County's greatest attractions for San Franciscans. In fact,

The Junction House in San Bruno was a typical hotel/restaurant of the early twentieth century. Built at the junction of County Road and the San Bruno Toll Road by San Francisco restaurateur August Jeneivin in 1889, the structure contained a restaurant and bar, with sleeping accommodations on the second floor. Junction House went through several changes of ownership but continued to function as a tavern until the 1920s. It was razed in the mid-1930s. Courtesy, San Mateo County Historical Association Archives

The original streetcar line running from San Francisco to the peninsula followed the Mission Road and extended to Baden (present-day South San Francisco) by 1893. Courtesy, San Mateo County Historical Association Archives

when the San Francisco and San Mateo Railroad Company began planning its streetcar route in 1890, it called for the line to follow the Mission Road through the cemeteries. By 1893 the line had reached Baden (part of today's South San Francisco), but it did not extend to San Mateo until almost 10 years later. One of the cemeteries, Mount Olivet, went so far as to establish its own spur line in 1896 in order to make its facilities off the road more accessible.

The San Francisco and San Mateo Railroad Company responded to the brisk traffic to the cemeteries by creating a unique car called the Cypress Lawn, which was

Auto racing at Tanforan was popular in the first years of the century. Later, autos racing against airplanes gained some popularity; the autos usually won, due to the airplanes' inability to make the tight turns required to be competitive. Courtesy, Herman S. Hoyt Collection, California Historical Society, San Francisco

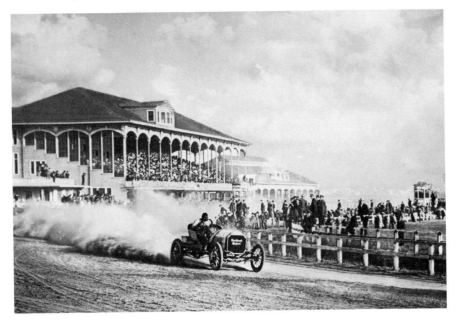

expressly designed to carry funeral parties to Colma. This ornate vehicle was comparatively small. It contained a special compartment for a casket and wicker chairs for the mourners. United Railroads bought the right to operate the line in 1902 and constructed three more funeral cars between 1903 and 1904. These cars were elaborately built to suit their distinctive purpose. Painted Brewster green with red roofs and gold lettering, they featured luxuriously cushioned seats, richly carpeted floors, dark window drapes, and beautiful woodwork. Lead inserts were attached to their wheels and gears in order to cut down on noise. Divided into three compartments, these 45-foot-long, 43,000-pound, 32-seat streetcars were always maintained in immaculate condition and became the ultimate in style for carrying the dead to their final resting places.

East of the cemeteries, the county's only industrial town was formed, again because of the proximity to San Francisco. In 1887 cattle baron Charles Lux died, and his lands went up for sale. One year later G.F. Swift visited the area and liked the prospect of creating a Pacific Coast meat packing center there. In addition to being close to the city, Swift noted that the place had good access to both rail and oceangoing transportation. It also was situated where the wind could carry the offensive fumes of the slaughterhouses out over the bay.

Swift planned to convince all the large Chicago meat packing firms to establish a joint stockyard to serve future nearby plants. Meanwhile, toward the west, a residential community would be created for the workers.

In 1891 Swift organized the South San Francisco Land and Improvement Company to promote the endeavor. Fierce opposition developed, however, from established butchers in San Francisco. Most of Swift's potential backers chose not to get involved at this point, but the entrepreneur carried on anyway. In 1892 the stockyards were completed and a plant called the Western Meat Company began operations. After it proved successful, the Armour Company joined Swift. Also attracted to the industrial town were manufacturers of paint and steel.

During the nineteenth century the lands south of South San Francisco were rural. Several roadhouses were present that catered to a transient population of gamblers, hunters, and other sportsmen.

The most notable occurrence in this area was the development of 120 acres by the Western Turf Association for use as a horse track. Polish Prince Andre Pontiatowski financed the undertaking. The track, named Tanforan, opened for business in 1899.

In 1902 the California Jockey Club bought the track from the prince for $82,000. The club, which had varying degrees of success with the enterprise during its first season, leased it to the California

The first homes built for refugees of the San Francisco earthquake were small dwellings known as "refugee shacks." Some of these were built in San Francisco after the quake and transported south to sites in Daly City and other north county cities. This 1906 refugee shack stood at 224 Los Olivos in Daly City until it was removed in 1971 to make room for the Daly City BART station and tracks. Courtesy, Samuel C. Chandler History Collection, Daly City

Auto Club in 1903. Car racing at Tanforan became extremely popular, with speeds reaching in excess of 60 miles per hour. In 1908 interest dropped off dramatically when betting was outlawed at all tracks in California.

For a while Tanforan's major attraction shifted to air shows. Races between automobiles and planes pulled in huge crowds. During World War I the military used Tanforan as a training field. It reopened as a track in 1923. No betting was allowed, and it only lasted two seasons. Finally, in 1933, pari-mutuel betting became legal, and John Marchbank of Daly City again opened the track, this time quite successfully until the outbreak of World War II.

The presence of San Francisco had much to do with the unique way in which the north county evolved. It has served as an amusement park for adults, complete with saloons and horsetracks, and as a source of farm and dairy products. It has been a primary location as a burial ground for the crowded city to the north. No aspect of San Francisco history had more impact, however, than the Great Earthquake and Fire of 1906.

As refugees streamed across the county line, Daly and other dairymen offered shelter and donated food. Almost immediately it dawned on many north county landowners that at least a portion of these people might want to make new homes away from the ruins of the city. In 1907 Daly became one of the first to capitalize upon the refugees' need for shelter by breaking up his dairy and selling housing lots for $200 to $300 each. In those days houses could be built for as little as $1,500 apiece on the lots. Some new

residents had the remnants of burned out houses dragged from San Francisco to the north county for a few hundred dollars and then fixed them up as new homes.

As the new housing tracts bloomed, there developed fears that San Francisco might try to annex the north county. In 1908 a proposal therefore was made to create one large city to be called Vista Grande. This would have included all of present-day Daly City, Colma, Brisbane, South San Francisco and Pacifica. However, many local people opposed this idea. They cited the different characteristics of the region—residential to the west, industrial to the east, and still rural to the south. South San Francisco independently ended any dreams of uniting this section of the county by incorporating as a town in 1908. Daly City followed in 1911—taking the name of the self-made dairyman who remained on three acres of his original 250-acre ranch.

In San Bruno, which had been little more than a railroad stop before the earthquake, lots quickly sold for as little as $225 each, payable in $5 monthly installments. The muddy roads of the instant town demanded improvement. San Bruno incorporated in 1914 to answer this need and to provide other services.

South of San Bruno, there was not the same activity. This was due to the presence of the Mills estate and the family's reluctance to sell its properties. The Millbrae area did experience development after World War I, but it did not incorporate as a town until 1946.

In the area just northeast of Mount San Bruno, developers hoped to create a San Bruno type of success, but, like Millbrae, the area

grew slowly. Not until 1961 did Brisbane incorporate.

MID-COUNTY AREA

The mid-county area's history was, for decades, largely the story of the Howard family and its extensions. The reader may remember that W.D.M. Howard and his partner, Henry Mellus, purchased the Rancho San Mateo in 1846. This property, which included northern San Mateo and most of Hillsborough and Burlingame, was obtained for $25,000 or about $4 an acre.

Howard, the son of a well-to-do New England seafaring family, went to sea in 1824 at the age of 16. He came to California in 1839 and

settled in Los Angeles as a clerk. There he married Mary Warren of Hawaii, who was on her return trip from a Boston school. Unfortunately the young bride died shortly after the wedding. In 1845 Howard joined with Mellus to create a mercantile firm. The two were in the right place, doing the right thing, at the right time, and they made a fortune supplying goods to the gold seekers of 1849. In that same year Howard married again. This time

Left: The home of W.D.M. Howard, El Cerrito, is an example of the Carpenter Gothic architectural style, with steep pointed gables, gingerbread bargeboards, a square tower, and a veranda. The home was named for a small hill just north of it (now called "The Mounds"). El Cerrito stood on what is now De Sabla Road in San Mateo, just west of El Camino Real and north of Baywood. Courtesy, San Mateo County Historical Association Archives

Below: The sitting room of W.D.M. Howard's El Cerrito attests to the opulence of the large estates built on the peninsula in the late nineteenth and early twentieth centuries. Courtesy, The Howard Collection, San Mateo County Historical Association Archives

Agnes Poett was the object of his affections. She had been stranded on board a ship in San Francisco Bay after the vessel's crew abandoned their duties in favor of searching for gold.

By 1850 Howard had made enough money to retire with his young bride to Rancho San Mateo. Mellus was bought out of his share of the property, and Howard had a fine prefabricated home erected on his land, which was called "El Cerrito." During his time there, Howard introduced the first high-grade cattle to California. He died at the age of 48 in 1856.

To his 25-year-old wife, Howard left the southern half of his rancho. He willed the northern half to Agnes' father, Dr. Joseph Henry Poett. The doctor, in turn, bestowed the western portion of his holdings on his other daughter, Julia (Mrs. John Redington).

William Davis Merry Howard was born in Boston in 1819. Arriving in California in 1839, he purchased Rancho San Mateo in the 1840s and constructed one of the county's first large homes, El Cerrito. Howard built the structure from prefabricated parts brought around Cape Horn from Boston by ship. Courtesy, San Mateo County Historical Association Archives

Here the family lived in beauty and comfort for many years. Agnes married W.D.M.'s brother, George Howard, outlived him, and was married a third time to Henry Bowie in 1870. John Redington became known as Burlingame's first commuter. In the 1860s he had a small train station constructed at the current site of the Oak Grove depot. It was commonly referred to as the "pill box" station.

In 1866 Dr. Poett sold diplomat and adventurer Anson Burlingame 1,000 acres for $52,000. Much of this property is included in today's Burlingame and Hillsborough. Burlingame had been the United States minister to China but switched allegiance to become a subject of the emperor of China. As such he negotiated the famous Burlingame Treaty, which permitted the importation of Chinese coolie labor into the United States for construction of the transcontinental railroad. For these services Burlingame earned a fortune. On his newly acquired peninsula land, he hoped to create a large planned community after the English country style, which allowed for the building of substantial cottages in an exclusively residential setting, with winding roads and much space between homes for recreational pursuits. Burlingame died in 1870 before he could get a start on his dream. William C. Ralston then purchased the property.

Ralston came to California in 1853 as an agent for a New York shipping line. In 1864 he organized the Bank of California and came to believe in Burlingame's planned community idea for the attractive 1,000 acre tract. He went so far as to publish a map for the community, which he called "Ralstonville." But in 1875

Ralston's financial world collapsed around him. His body was found floating in the bay one day in August—perhaps due to a swimming mishap, perhaps as a result of suicide. Ralston's longtime business associate, William Sharon, took over his position at the bank. In addition, as Ralston's largest creditor, Sharon obtained his San Mateo County properties and the Palace Hotel in San Francisco.

Sharon had come to California by wagon train in 1850. He was Ralston's agent to the Comstock Mining District in Nevada and made his own fortune in that role. Sharon also believed in Burlingame's dream and created a map of the area, but instead of calling the site Ralstonville, he gave it the name "Burlingame."

Although he tried, Sharon was unable to find buyers for the property and decided to sell the portion east of El Camino Real to William Corbitt, who established a successful ranch. On the remaining land he set up a dairy to supply the Palace Hotel. Sharon died in the midst of a scandal involving a woman named Sarah Althea Hill. Sharon's son-in-law, Francis Newlands, then took major responsibility for caring for the family assets.

Newlands had trained to become a lawyer in the East. In 1870 he came to California and was hired by Sharon. He later married his employer's daughter. Sharon was one of the wealthiest capitalists in California, and Newlands had much to do as defender of the family's interests. After his father-in-law's death, Newlands decided to straighten out many of the family's holdings by disposing of various properties. He targeted the selling of acreage in the Washington, D.C.,

San Francisco entrepreneur William C. Ralston built his home in present-day Belmont. Legend has it that Ralston delighted in inviting guests to dinner, placing them on the train from San Francisco to Belmont, and then racing the train from San Francisco in his horse-drawn carriage. He often arrived at the Belmont station before the train. Courtesy, San Mateo County Historical Association Archives

area and the Burlingame tract. For both he fell back upon the old idea of creating an exclusive country suburb. He succeeded with his eastern real estate first. There he promised potential buyers that he would establish a country club in the area after enough parties had bought into the community. This incentive worked, and when the designated number of investors had been reached, Newlands made good on his promise and created the Chevy Chase Country Club.

The concept of the country club was new. The first had only been organized five years previously, in 1885, at Brookline, Massachusetts. Its attraction for real estate buyers in the Chevy Chase area was not lost on Newlands. He felt a similiar success could be obtained in Burlingame, which was only 20 miles away from the West's most important city, with scores of wealthy people who could be interested in becoming charter members of the first country club to be formed west of the Mississippi.

In 1892 Newlands had six cottages constructed to begin sales. He then made the same offer to potential buyers that he had made to buyers in the East. This time, however, he could not find interested parties. Undaunted, Newlands decided to reverse the order of things by establishing the country club and then attracting buyers.

He persuaded 50 young men of ample means from San Francisco to form the club. In exchange, Newlands gave them use of one of the recently constructed cottages with furnishings and 20 acres of land free for two years. During this period the Palace Hotel provided all the supplies needed to maintain the clubhouse plus the services of a staff. Transportation from Oak Grove Station was furnished at 12 and one-half cents a trip. Finally, if things did not work out after two years and the club became indebted, the Sharon Estate would pay up to one half the loss. Thus was born the Burlingame Country Club in 1893.

The risk turned out to be a good one for Newlands, as the club did attract buyers to the area. For the club members, the recreational value of their new facilities and the country that surrounded them became a great boon. In 1894 they joined with the Southern Pacific Railroad in building a train station nearer to their clubhouse. Their Burlingame Station became the first permanent structure in California designed in the Mission Revival style of architecture. A small community, whose purpose was to cater to the needs of the country club set, developed around the train depot.

As the new century began, the club became increasingly popular with San Francisco's elite. The reputation of the place was not lost on those of lower social status, however. After the earthquake of 1906, many individuals came to the Burlingame area simply because they recognized the name. From a population of 200 in 1906, Burlingame swelled to 1,000 in one year. By 1910, 1,585 people lived there, and in 1914 there were 2,849.

This rapid increase dismayed the Burlingame Country Club's membership, which mostly lived among the hills west of El Camino.

The Burlingame Country Club's first home was a cottage built by Arthur Paige Brown. By the end of the nineteenth century, the original home of George Pope was the new clubhouse. Shortly thereafter a third clubhouse, designed by George Howard, replaced it. In 1912, after that facility was destroyed by fire, the clubhouse shown here was completed. This clubhouse was used until 1955, when the club moved into New Place, originally built by William Crocker as a country estate. Courtesy, San Mateo County Historical Association Archives

De Martini's wholesale and retail liquor store was located in San Mateo on Second Avenue, between Main and B streets, in the early twentieth century. The man in the suit in the foreground of this photo is Ad Baradat, agent for Wieland's Beer. Courtesy, San Mateo County Historical Association Archives

Pictured is the summer residence of the Tilton family, in what is now the city of San Mateo. The railroad and Coyote Point are both visible in the background. This residence stood east of the commercial region of San Mateo, and north of San Mateo Creek. When the estate was subdivided, the house itself was subdivided; a portion of the original home is still used as a residence on South Delaware Street. From Moore and DePue's Illustrated History of San Mateo County, 1878. Courtesy, San Mateo County Historical Association Archives

Alvinza Hayward was instrumental in the development of the city of San Mateo. Courtesy, San Mateo County Historical Association Archives

They feared that one of two towns to the east, Burlingame or San Mateo, might try to annex their properties. Burlingame itself had incorporated in 1908, feeling that San Mateo might try to annex it. Both towns had then taken in surrounding communities. San Mateo annexed San Mateo Park in 1909 and Hayward Park in 1910. Burlingame had added Easton to its territory in 1910.

With both towns eyeing the properties to the west, the club members were faced with the prospect of being regulated by a local government in which they would be a minority. Still worse, they would be obligated to pay taxes for the things they most wanted to avoid. Streets would be widened, sidewalks laid, commercialism and industry encouraged, hills leveled, and creeks filled. Arthur H. Redington rallied the members to create their own town and prevent these things from happening. The resi-

dents successfully incorporated Hillsborough in 1910.

East of Hillsborough and south of Burlingame, the community of San Mateo had by the 1890s become the leading town in the county. It had started as little more than a stagecoach stop, but its location halfway between San Francisco and San Jose, at the terminus of the road to Half Moon Bay, positioned it for growth.

When the San Francisco-San Jose Railroad was completed in 1864, one of its initial investors, Charles B. Polhemus, saw the value of promoting the sale of property in the San Mateo area. He decided to subdivide and sell 176 lots out of what had been a wheat field. In one year 40 lots were bought along B Street, which became San Mateo's main thoroughfare. By 1870, 90 percent of the lots had been purchased, and a town was in the making.

Early San Mateo was, however, boxed in by large estates on all sides. John Parrott and Stephen Whipple owned properties to the west, the Howards were, of course, to the north, and Alvinza Hayward's place was to the south and east.

Of all the large-estate owners, Hayward took the greatest interest in San Mateo. Known as a hard businessman, Hayward was famous for being the only man ever to better William Sharon in a deal. He had made his fortune as a gold miner, mill owner, investor in the Comstock, stockbroker, and real estate speculator. To the citizens of San Mateo, he was best known as a benefactor. He provided for the town's first water system and did much to create Central Park.

In 1889 C.M. Kirkbride and R.H.

Jury founded San Mateo's first newspaper, the *Leader,* and began advocating the town's incorporation. An election was held in 1894 in which 150 voted for and 25 voted against the measure. San Mateo thus became the county's second incorporated town.

San Mateo continued its moderate growth into the twentieth century, maintaining an image as a clean suburban town. In 1918, before Prohibition, San Mateans voted to close all of the saloons.

Prior to World War II the most important development shaping the future of San Mateo may have been the establishment of Bay Meadows Race Track by William P. Kyne in 1934. As with the reopening of Tanforan to the north, the legalization of pari-mutuel betting in California made the opening of the track possible. Bay Meadows became one of the county's greatest attractions. In its early years some of the most famous horses in the world ran there, including Seabiscuit, owned by Hillsborough's Charles S. Howard. A cadre of celebrities, including entertainment personalities from the southern part of the state, came to see the well-known horses.

SOUTH COUNTY

Simon Mezes, who acquired much of the best of the Arguello family's huge Rancho de las Pulgas, dominated the south county's early history.

Mezes arrived in California on February 22, 1850, at the age of 28. Evidence suggests that he had been president of a bank in Puerto Rico. In a short period of time, he recognized that his legal and financial background, coupled with his ability to read and write in two lan-

In 1867 Redwood City, the seat of county government, was the first municipality to incorporate. From a town of dirt roads and facilities supporting the logging and farming industry, it grew into a prosperous business area. Shown here is the Main Street of Redwood City in the 1920s. Courtesy, San Mateo County Historical Association Archives

guages, would enable him to start a legal practice defending the claims of the Mexican land grantees against squatters from the East.

Perhaps his most valued client was the Arguello family. Through his services as lawyer, agent, and then manager, he eventually came to own about a fourth of the Rancho de las Pulgas. His task in defending their ownership of the property against a host of squatters was formidable. In a shrewd transaction, Mezes sold a portion of the rancho to William Carey Jones, who happened to be a member of the United States Land Commission. Jones had been especially sent to California to

With the decline of the lumber industry in the late nineteenth century, farming became an important way of life in Redwood City. Shown here in an 1878 engraving is the farmhouse of Mrs. Caroline Hawes. From Moore and DePue's Illustrated History of San Mateo County, 1878. Courtesy, San Mateo County Historical Association Archives

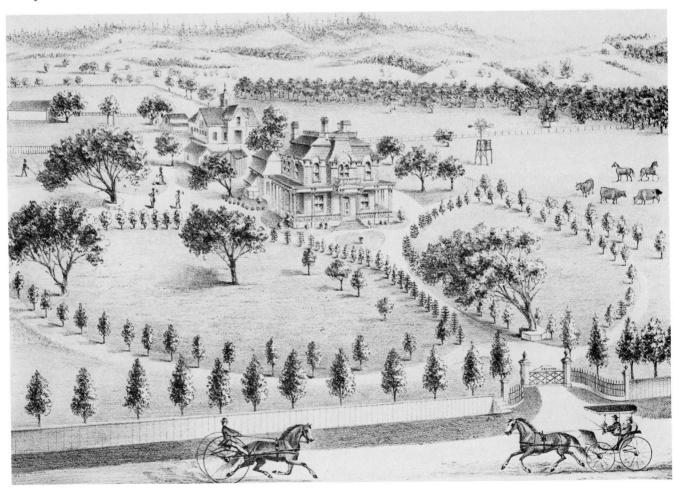

review the legality of various Mexican land grants. He was also important as powerful United States Senator Thomas Hart Benton's son-in-law and John C. Fremont's brother-in-law. Due to the sale, Jones had a direct interest in seeing the Arguellos' grant affirmed. Mezes in this way assured himself of at least one vote from the three-man commission and prevailed when the crucial decisions were made.

Part of the property Mezes came to own was the infant town springing up along the embarcadero in what is now known as Redwood City. After his success in defending the land grant, he surveyed the area and divided it into lots that he peddled to the squatters already present. His block and lot map determined the streets as they are still known in the downtown portion of Redwood City.

As can be guessed, the squatters were not thrilled with having to buy land they considered theirs already. Mezes irritated the locals still more by calling the place "Mezesville." Most of the townspeople reluctantly bought their lots for about $75 each. On the deeds some wrote that their purchases were part of the "so-called town of Mezesville." When the post office was established in 1856, they chose the name "Redwood City." The other appellation faded from memory.

Because Redwood City was the only town on the bay side in those early years it was selected to become county seat in 1856. Business activity centered around Broadway. In many ways Redwood City resembled a typical town of the West. The dirt streets were either dusty or muddy, depending upon the season. Sidewalks were made of

planks of wood. On occasion the place could be rough and wild, especially when the loggers came to town.

By the middle 1860s the hamlet's character began to change to a more law-abiding, family-oriented community. The metamorphosis occurred as a result of both the decline in the logging industry, which had encouraged the presence of single transient men, and the rise of farming, which demanded the existence of a town devoted to serving family-operated farms. The completion of the San Francisco-San Jose Railroad in 1864 also had an impact.

In 1867 Redwood City became the first municipality to incorporate in San Mateo County. It thus gained the ability to impose taxes in order to pave streets, create a water system, install gas lighting, and build a bridge across the creek. Throughout most of the nineteenth century, Redwood City was the

most populous town in the county. It grew from 400 in 1860 to 700 in 1870 and to almost 1,400 in 1880.

Unlike other parts of the bay side that were dominated by San Francisco's elite, in Redwood City development was controlled by the town's small businessmen. Locals also became involved in county politics and tended to exert much more influence in local matters than other county residents well into the present century.

While Mezes was active in the creation of Redwood City, he actually lived in the Belmont area until his death in 1884 at age 62. Well before that, in 1854, Mezes sold a portion of his Belmont property to the Italian nobleman, Leonetto Cipriani. Here Cipriani built a fine home and lived for 10 years. In 1864 Cipriani's old friend, Victor Emmanuel, became king of Italy, and Cipriani decided to return to his native country. He then sold his estate to

William Ralston purchased and enlarged the Cipriani Estate, using it as the basis for his own mansion. In 1922 the mansion became part of the College of Notre Dame in Belmont, and was renamed Ralston Hall. On the main floor, the interior has been restored. In this 1950 photo, the original Cipriani portion of the building is at the right—part of the east wing. Courtesy, San Mateo County Historical Association Archives

Timothy Guy Phelps made his home in San Carlos, buying 3,500 acres of land there. Phelps served in both the state legislature and the U.S. Congress. Courtesy, San Mateo County Historical Association Archives

Morton Cheesman for $5,500. Three days later, Cheesman found this a profitable purchase, as William Ralston bought it from him for $6,500. Ralston used parts of the original Cipriani house for building a huge 50-bedroom mansion. In a manner similar to what took place in Burlingame, the estate later came into the hands of William Sharon. The home eventually became part of today's College of Notre Dame.

While Cipriani, Ralston, and Sharon gave Belmont an air of distinction, the place was much better known for Carl Janke's Belmont Park. Thousands of picnickers visited it by railroad from the late 1860s until the turn of the century. The park was fashioned as sort of a German beer garden. Records show parties of 8,000 and more were present there for various colorful ethnic occasions. Unfortunately, drunken brawls, murders, and kidnappings gave the spot a bad reputation, and local citizens eventually pressured the railroad into curtailing its special service.

Belmont slowly grew to be a small town. Fearing annexation by booming San Carlos to the south, it incorporated in 1927.

San Carlos originated as Timothy Guy Phelps' dream. At the age of 25, Phelps came to California with the great 1849 migration of gold seekers. He found no gold in the hills but became a successful merchant in San Francisco. While engaged in the grain business, he discovered the fertile lands of the San Carlos area and eventually bought up 3,500 acres there. Phelps was an important leader in his day. He served in the state legislature and the United States Congress, and became a close friend of Abraham Lincoln. He twice ran for governor of California and was a regent of the University of California for 19 years. Phelps is also distinguished for having founded the Bank of Redwood City, the county's first financial institution. He was killed in 1899 when he was accidentally run down by a tandem bicycle.

Long before the freak incident that ended his life, Phelps believed a city could be brought into being in the San Carlos area. In 1887 formal plans were drawn, a railroad station was built, and lots went up for sale. Unfortunately for Phelps and other investors involved in the project, only about a dozen families came to live there.

In fact San Carlos developed very slowly throughout the nineteenth century and into the twentieth. While many towns on the peninsula had big spurts in population growth after the earthquake, San Carlos did not. Only after World War I and the entrance of skilled promoter Fred Drake onto the scene did San Carlos expand. Extraordinarily, Drake had San Carlos growing at a faster rate than any other community in California during the 1920s. The town was incorporated in 1925.

South of Redwood City the estates of the elite again dominated the landscape. In 1860 the wealthy hide-and-tallow businessman from Chile, Faxon Atherton, bought 600 acres of Pulgas property north of today's Menlo Park and called his great summer home "Valparaiso." This became the first of the great south county mansions. Soon prominent capitalist James C. Flood and others joined the Atherton family, and, until the creation of the Burlingame Country Club in 1893, this was the most popular section of the county for the upper class.

South from Valparaiso, the Menlo Park train station was established in 1867. A dozen businesses sprang up around it, and the community incorporated as a town in 1874. Political pressure from estate owners and farmers in the area forced disincorporation, however, in 1876.

Menlo Park had a rough charac-

ter in its younger years. Its reputation proved potent enough to encourage Leland and Jane Stanford to found their college south of the county line in 1891.

During World War I Menlo Park became the site of Camp Fremont, the training center for thousands of recruits. The military post's history began in 1917, when the Army leased 25 acres and then spent $1,900,000 on improvements. More than 27,000 soldiers were housed at the camp at one time.

After the war Menlo Park felt the need to incorporate again, and this time wished to include the wealthy area of Fair Oaks. As the residents of Hillsborough had done before, the estate owners wished to retain their exclusiveness and incorporated their area as the town of Atherton. This removed from the residents of Menlo Park much of the incentive for creating a formal municipality. Finally, in 1927, the town organized.

In the areas west and east of Menlo Park and Atherton, growth was slow until World War II.

Left: *James Flood, saloon keeper-turned-stockbroker and mining tycoon, moved to Menlo Park in the 1880s. He built a six-story mansion named Linden Towers and lived there until his death in 1889. The mansion changed ownership several times, then was bought back by Flood's son. Courtesy, San Mateo County Historical Association Archives*

Below: *In the mid- and late nineteenth century, Belmont Park was a favorite spot for picnics and social gatherings. In this photograph, an unidentified group posed in the park. Courtesy, San Mateo County Historical Association Archives*

Toward the hills the Woodside area lost population after the logging industry declined in the 1860s. Dr. Tripp's Woodside Store continued to operate until 1909, but the center of the community shifted to the intersection of Woodside and Canada roads. By the 1880s the place had a couple of stores, at least three saloons, and a hotel. The character of Woodside began to change in the early 1900s, when business leaders August Schilling and James Folger established homes there.

South of Woodside, in the Portola Valley, farming and stock ranching predominated until well after the turn of the century. Englishman Andrew Hallidie was the most famous early resident. With his invention of the cable railroad in the late 1860s, he forever influenced the character of the City of San Francisco. In 1883 Hallidie bought property in Portola Valley. He donated land for the creation of a school and post office, which became the nucleus of the small community. From his home Hallidie staged experiments with cable transportation, constructing a model tramway that ran from the valley floor into the mountains.

On the bay side of Menlo Park, the Ravenswood area remained rural after the business failure of Isaiah Woods in 1854. While the earthquake of 1906 had little effect on the area, Ravenswood did change after the turn of the century. Berry farms and Japanese flower-growing enterprises replaced wheat fields, and in 1909 Charles Weeks started a successful poultry ranch.

Weeks had a great interest in social reform. In 1916 he made 600 acres available to the socialist movement of William Smythe for

Above: *Linden Towers, the mansion built by James Flood in the 1880s, was a Carpenter Gothic construction often referred to as "Flood's Wedding Cake." One of the most ornate examples of this architectural style on the peninsula, the mansion was demolished in 1934 and the property subdivided. This photograph was taken by noted San Francisco photographer Gabriel Moulin. Courtesy, San Mateo County Historical Association Archives, from the San Mateo County Curriculum Department*

Facing page, top: *Though disincorporated in 1876, Menlo Park retained its identity. This 1888 photograph shows the Menlo Parlor of the Native Sons (and Daughters) of the Golden West. Courtesy, San Mateo County Historical Association Archives*

Facing page, bottom: *M.J. Doyle's general merchandise store in Menlo Park was one of the businesses which developed with the coming of the railroad. As in the mid-county area, businesses catering to the needs of estate owners and local farmers formed the nucleus for the development of incorporated cities. From Moore & DePue's* Illustrated History of San Mateo County, 1878. *Courtesy, San Mateo County Historical Association Archives*

creation of the colony of Runnymede (one of five communes established by Smythe in California). The experimental utopian community consisted of as many as 900 individuals by 1925, and plans were made to incorporate. Many in the area wanted Ravenswood annexed to Palo Alto, however, and others wished it to remain unorganized. After a special election residents agreed that the place would receive a new name, East Palo Alto, but no move was made to create a formal municipality or join with Palo Alto. Runnymede disappeared in the 1930s, and the area remained sparsely populated until the 1940s.

THE COAST SIDE

The central theme of the coast side's history is isolation. With San Pedro Mountain to the north, the coastal mountains to the east, the chalklike cliffs of Santa Cruz County to the south, and the Pacific Ocean (without an adequate natural harbor) to the west, residents of the coast side have long been sealed into their section of the county. The result has been that the Coast has stayed mostly rural.

However, there have been plenty of attempts to break this isolation. As early as 1855 a road was graded to connect Half Moon Bay to San Mateo. It essentially became the coast side's most utilized land route during the nineteenth century. From Half Moon Bay, it took two days for a farmer to get his produce to San Francisco by horse-drawn wagon—a long and arduous trip.

Some did try to get to the San Francisco market by sea. In 1864, at Point Ano Nuevo, William Waddell built a 700-foot wharf to connect his shingle mill, located five miles up Waddell Creek, with oceangoing vessels. By 1867 craft docking at the wharf were transporting 2,000,000 feet of lumber a year from Waddell's mill and others in the area. For a decade this was the most important shipping station on the San Mateo coast. Both Waddell's enterprise and his life ended in 1875 when he was attacked by a grizzly bear.

North of Ano Nuevo a crane-and-cable system was built at Pigeon Point. This met with limited success since, while ships waited for the cargo to come slowly on board, they stood offshore in a perilous rolling sea with rocks on all sides.

Farmer Alexander Gordon may have conducted the most interesting experiment to overcome the isolation of the coast side. In 1872 he built a chute from the bluffs on the north side of Tunitas Creek that connected with the ocean below. Gordon felt that this might be both the answer for transporting produce from his 1,000 acre farm to market and the salvation of other farmers in the area.

Gordon constructed the more than 100-foot chute at a 45 degree angle, which presented problems. The friction from the downward trip burned holes in sacks of potatoes and grain, and, if they were not already on fire on the way down, the sacks sometimes burst when they finally hit the deck of the waiting ship.

The huge Pacific swells and rocks just off the bluff represented a still greater hindrance. Ships' captains wisely refused to load except under the most calm conditions. Depressed farm prices during the middle 1870s also hurt Gordon, and he eventually went bankrupt. In 1885 a storm destroyed the chute, but the original eyebolts can still be seen.

Perhaps the oldest embarcadero on the coast side existed in Mexican times near Half Moon Bay at Miramar. During the latter part of the nineteenth century, it was called Amesport after its owner, J.P. Ames. This pier was most successful during the 1890s. Local newspapers noted that the vessel, *Gypsy,* sailed every Friday for Half Moon Bay with supplies from San Francisco. On its return trip to the city, *Gypsy* might carry grain, hay, or potatoes.

Ames himself became a powerful local politician. He served as a county supervisor, and during the years when he was active, the coastal section became more influential politically than at any other time in its history. Ames eventually left the coast side when he accepted an appointment as warden of San Quentin Prison.

Despite the good work of the *Gypsy,* Amesport was still not protected or large enough to fulfill all the transportation needs of the coast side. Meanwhile, produce from this section was becoming more valuable, as dairy ranching and vegetable growing replaced grain and potato farming.

In order to break the isolation of the coast side once and for all, a group of influential men formed the Ocean Shore Railroad Company on May 18, 1905. The idea was to link San Francisco and Santa Cruz with an electric, two-track railroad, buy up the real estate on both sides of the tracks, and watch the land values grow. In addition they would address the needs of the local farmers and allow for the exploitation of the untouched timber and mineral resources of the coast side.

These planners were well respected and substantial individuals. J. Downey Harvey, an important San Francisco banker, served as the first president of the company. J.A. Folger, the coffee king, became one of the vice presidents. Another vice president was Horace D. Pillsbury of the important law firm of Pillsbury, Madison and Sutro. Peter D. Martin, a member of the pioneer California family, and Charles C. Moore, president of a large engineering company, were both directors.

These organizers recognized that there were grave problems to overcome. The coast side's gullies would require numerous bridges. At many points just below San Francisco, construction would have to take place 200 to 300 feet above the surf. The worst obstacles centered around Mount San Pedro. A 400-foot tunnel through it would empty out on a narrow ledge 700 feet above the Pacific. Known as Devil's Slide, this ledge already was recognized as being unstable.

Despite the company's knowledge of these risks, it began construction in 1905 from both ends of the line. It made good progress until April 18, 1906. The San Francisco earthquake caused significant damage. At Mussel Rock, 4,000 feet of track, along with rolling stock and construction equipment, was knocked into the ocean. This hurt the principal stockholders, and, since their losses were not only in the Ocean Shore Railroad but also in various parts of San Francisco, reinvestment was extremely difficult. In order to immediately mitigate the damage, plans were downgraded. The double track line was changed to single track, and the electric rail idea gave way to steam engines. In May the company actually earned revenue as the line between Santa Cruz and Swanton went into operation. Unfortunately for the Ocean Shore Railroad, a competing line was laid right next to its southern track. This was

bought in 1907 by the Southern Pacific, which quickly captured the important cement works business at Davenport.

Despite all the setbacks, work continued on the northern end of the line. Remarkably, the crucial construction was completed around the Devil's Slide area. To create the 400 foot tunnel through Mount San Pedro, 3,500 tons of solid rock had to be removed. To bring this about, a small tunnel 70 feet long was driven into the mountain. For three days it was stuffed with nine tons of black powder. The larger tunnel was then blown into existence. It emptied out 700 feet above the rocky shoreline, where laborers laid track on a cut in the cliff.

As work approached Devil's Slide, the railroad's subsidiary, the Ocean Shore Land Company, went into action. The company expected that real estate sales would be good. It hoped victims of the earthquake would want to escape the perils of living in San Francisco by moving to the coast side, just as they had gone to Daly City and other locations on the peninsula.

For a while it looked like the idea might work. Five future communities were laid out; they were called Edgemar, Salada Beach, Brighton Beach, Vellemar, and San Pedro Terrace (the beginnings of what would eventually become the city of Pacifica). An energetic promotional campaign offered train excursions to the properties, which were met by brass bands, free lunches, and multilingual company representatives. Lots sold, hotels were planned, and some even placed improvements on their new properties.

It was at this time that Henry

The Troutmere Guernsey Farm, pictured here circa 1940, is typical of the coast side of San Mateo County even today. The coastal portion of the county retains its rural character, with a few small towns serving the needs of the predominantly agricultural area to the south, although there is increased population and residential growth in Half Moon Bay. Courtesy, San Mateo County Historical Association Archives

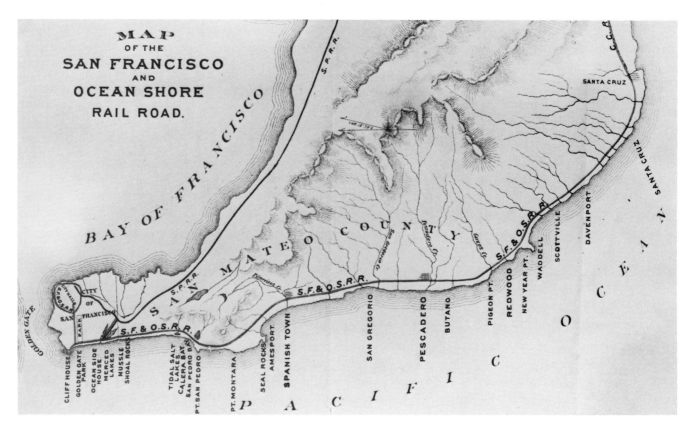

This early twentieth century map shows the proposed route of the Ocean Shore Railroad, which, had it been successful, would have changed the character of the coast side from predominantly rural to residential. Difficulties in construction and the success of the Bayside rail development shifted population growth to the eastern part of the county. Courtesy, San Mateo County Historical Association Archives

Harrison McCloskey built the Salada Beach castle. After the 1906 disaster, McCloskey decided to move his family out of the city. He established two new homes, one in San Carlos and the other, which still looks like a medieval castle, at Salada Beach on the side of a hill overlooking the ocean. Henry's son, Paul N. McCloskey, attended Lowell High School and commuted on the Ocean Shore Railroad. Pete McCloskey, Henry's grandson, became a United States congressman. Henry died in 1914, and the family sold the castle. In the 1920s it periodically surfaced in the news as an abortion clinic, speakeasy, and signalling station for rum runners. During World War II it was used as a lookout position for the coast artillery.

With the initial interest in land

came a huge demand for passenger service, and the Ocean Shore Railroad ran at capacity. In fact, at one point, flat cars with benches mounted on them were used to transport the throngs.

As success seemed in hand in the north, communities were planned further down the line at Montara, Moss Beach, Princeton, and Miramar. The greatest plans were, however, reserved for El Granada. Here the principal owners of the company invested their own money in subdivisions. Nationally renowned architect D.H. Burnham conceived the layout of the town, which was pronounced the future Coney Island of San Francisco.

Amazingly, 1,727 lots, worth $976,779, were sold at El Granada alone. Additional lots sold for

$5,795,384. Still, although everyone was buying, few were building. With this inactivity, lot owners who were actually speculating recognized a bubble that was about to burst. They ceased making payments on their investments, and the properties reverted to the company.

The real problem faced by the Ocean Shore Railroad was that the city of San Francisco was being rebuilt at an incredible rate. Real land values remained there. Thus in 1908, when the railroad attempted to float a $1,357,115 bond issue to complete only 26 more miles of track, there existed little interest. Incredibly, although the company had finished the most difficult part of the construction and had completed 54 of the 80 miles of track, the last gap could not be bridged.

Despite its short life, the Ocean Shore Railroad stimulated some growth on the coast side of San Mateo County. Establishments such as the Hotel El Granada catered to sightseers, as well as those seeking to purchase land in one of the many new developments created after 1906. Though the railroad ran from San Francisco to Tunitas Creek until 1920, the expected coast side land boom did not take place; to this day, San Mateo's coast is its most sparsely populated area. Courtesy, San Mateo County Historical Association Archives

Until 1920 the Ocean Shore Railroad continued in operation as a minor business that ran trains to Tunitas Creek. Then it completely stopped service. The popularity of the automobile made it unnecessary.

For the coast side, an adequate answer to the isolation problem has not been found to this day. During the 1930s the Cabrillo Highway was put through Devil's Slide, but its instability and narrowness have rendered it unacceptable to many as the solution—if, indeed, there is any solution short of major changes to the landscape.

THE BAY LANDS

During the nineteenth century San Mateo County had a substantial maritime industry. However, it did

Following the earthquake, coast side towns of San Francisco were targeted for residential development. In the early part of the century both sightseers and prospective landowners made the trek south on the Ocean Shore Railroad to view ocean property. This photo was taken at San Pedro Point about 1910. Courtesy, San Mateo County Historical Association Archives

While the Ocean Shore Railroad operated, county residents traveled on it to picnic spots along the San Mateo coast. Here, in an early twentieth century photo, members of the Greenleaf Club pose in contemporary beachwear. Courtesy, Samuel C. Chandler History Collection, Daly City

not exist on the coast side, where there were but two whaling stations and not much else. In his 1880 survey David Starr Jordon of the United States Commission of Fish and Fisheries located on the entire shoreline only one Portuguese and ten others "who fish when they can find nothing else to do." Jordon cited the coast side's inaccessibility to markets, a subject covered in the last section, as the reason for the scarcity of fishermen. As late as 1904 federal researchers found that the entire catch of the coast side was a 75,000-pound abalone harvest conducted by two men at Pigeon Point, who earned $2,500 for their efforts.

On the bay side of the peninsula, a very different story can be told. Here oyster gathering and shrimp fishing had international importance. Salt and cement making also became significant activities.

The oyster industry started in 1872, when Samuel J. Purseglove purchased underwater lands surrounding an old wreck known as Corville's Hulk, which lay north of the Seventeen Mile Slough off of today's Millbrae. From this location Purseglove became the first to plant eastern seed oysters off the San Mateo County bayline. Eastern oysters had a better taste than their smaller, grittier cousins of the Cali-

fornia estuaries, and this was the day when the oyster was the most important marketable marine food resource in the world. The transcontinental railroad had made transportation of the eastern seeds to the West Coast possible in 1867. Soon after Purseglove planted the seeds, the San Mateo County bay lands became the most productive in the Bay Area for the growing of oysters. This was because these underwater holdings had the greatest protection from the annual floods that created silty waters harmful to the delectable mollusks.

Purseglove's initial success was not unnoticed by the veteran oysterman John Stillwell Morgan. He acquired most of the bay lands off San Mateo County, including Purseglove's property, and became known as the man who perfected the "California Method" of oyster production.

The California Method had several interesting characteristics. Because oysters could not reproduce in the bay, Morgan had an average of one hundred boxcar loads of seed oysters shipped from the eastern beds annually. These seeds were about the size of a dime when they were placed on underwater lands off Belmont. Here the oystermen allowed them to grow for two years, then plucked the shellfish out of the bay and sent them to beds off Millbrae, where the tidal action was greater and more food was present for the oysters. After another two years, an oyster grew to about six inches in size and was ready for market.

The Morgan Oyster Company developed into an extremely successful business. After its beginnings in 1874, it earned hundreds of thousands of dollars and became the sole source of oysters for the western slope of North America. In the peak year, 1897, more than a million dollars worth of oysters were gathered. The industry's profitability dropped off considerably during the early twentieth century due to increased pollution of the bay. In 1923 the Morgan Oyster Company sold its holdings to the Pacific Portland Cement Company.

Not only did completion of the transcontinental railroad make possible the creation of the oyster industry, but it also spawned the shrimp fishing business. When the Chinese railroad builders found themselves released from their jobs, they many times sought work in the occupations they had known in China. Many from the southern provinces had been fishermen. Various discriminatory laws kept the Chinese from netting most catches, so they turned to shrimp fishing, where limited white competition existed.

"China camps" were established all around San Francisco Bay. These camps were actually small villages stationed to support the shrimp fleets. The first in San Mateo County was established in 1869 near Redwood City. The largest in the county was located off San Bruno Point. By 1880 it had developed into the most productive camp in California. Here, 24 men with 12 junks and 100 nets practiced their trade.

During the 1890s, the most productive decade, each boat averaged catches of 7,000 pounds of shrimp per day during the season. Half the haul was boiled and sold fresh in San Francisco. The remainder was boiled, salted, dried until hard, and crushed. The meat was then separated from the shell. The dried meat was sold as food and the shell used as fertilizer after exportation to China.

While pollution also gradually weakened this industry, the shrimp camps were actually driven out of business in 1915, when the state of California banned the use of the Chinese fisherman's favorite tool, the bag net.

At the turn of the century, as the oyster and shrimp businesses began to decline, a salt industry developed on the bay lands. Several companies began operating almost simultaneously in the Redwood City area. However, a single plant south of San Mateo made the most auspicious start.

C.E. Whitney, a former employee of east bay salt king August Schilling, created his salt ponds and built his plant near today's Delaware Street and Highway 92. Operations began in 1903. The company was originally called the C.E. Whitney Company, but Whitney soon changed the name to the Leslie Salt Refining Company to honor an uncle.

By 1907 the salt companies of the Redwood City area had merged with their northern counterpart and taken on a new title, the Leslie Salt Company. For the west bay salt makers, and particularly the Whitney family and the San Mateo plant, the next 15 years represented a golden period. In 1910 the San Mateo refinery became the first on the West Coast to install the vacuum refining method essential to the production of finer table salts. The Whitneys also developed the cylinder-shaped container, advertised as stronger and more protected than boxes.

In 1924 the east bay salt interests merged with Leslie. For reasons of economy the San Mateo plant was closed in 1931. Because the name "Leslie" was well-known due to the hard work of the Whitneys in advertising, packaging, and refinement methodology, the company retained it during its final consolidation and organization in 1936. Today's Leslie facilities in Redwood City were established in 1950. They represent the last vestige of this great San Mateo County enterprise.

While salt production in San Mateo County is not as important as it once was, the cement industry is still a vital force. It was initiated by educator, businessman, and Red-

This is one of the few extant photographs of the late nineteenth century shrimp fishing village that existed at Point San Bruno. Much of the catch was sold in San Francisco, but some was dried and shipped to China, where the meat was sold as food and the shells were used as fertilizer. Courtesy, Fish and Wildlife Service Archives, San Francisco Maritime Museum

wood City Mayor George A. Merrill. As organizer of the Redwood City Harbor Company, his firm was responsible for dredging operations in 1913. As work began, Merrill observed that vast quantities of fossilized oyster shell were present. Various studies found that the makeup of this shell was perfect for the manufacture of cement. Interest in the resource culminated in the establishment of the Pacific Portland Cement Company's plant at Redwood City. It is best known for providing the cement used to build the San Mateo-Hayward Bridge in 1929.

THE WATERSHED

Today's watershed was once a land of farms and small communities. San Francisco's need for fresh water, however, necessitated dramatic changes.

Originally San Francisco depended upon well water from the Presidio as a water supply. As the city grew in the 1850s, this source proved inadequate. For a time water had to be shipped across the bay in barrels.

In 1858 the Spring Valley Water Company incorporated to create reservoirs in San Mateo County as a resource for the city. By 1900 the company possessed 20,000 acres of peninsula property, located in areas ranging from the San Andreas Valley to San Francisco.

German-born, Swiss-trained engineer Herman Schussler masterminded the creation of the great lakes that now dominate the landscape of the middle section of the county. He designed a series of dams to accomplish this. The first, the Pilarcitos earthen dam, was constructed during the mid-1860s. This was followed by the completion of San Andreas Dam in 1868. In 1877 Upper Crystal Springs Lake was created. In 1879 the town of Searsville was flooded to form a lake (unfortunately, Searsville Lake was later found not to be needed). Schussler's greatest achievement was the building of Crystal Springs Dam. Started in 1887, this 150-foot-high engineering marvel was constructed with concrete interlocking blocks and was the largest of its kind in the world when finished in 1890. The completion of this dam resulted in the creation of lower Crystal Springs Lake. In order to bring it into being, the resort community of Crystal Springs, many farms, and the old Half Moon Bay Road were flooded.

To establish its reservoir system, the Spring Valley Water Company frequently enlisted the aid of the courts to remove people who lived in the valleys. The law judged that the needs of the City of San Francisco were more important than the rights of these individuals. Sometimes lands were condemned and then bought by the company for only 10 percent of their actual value.

While the Spring Valley Water Company became unpopular in certain quarters in San Mateo County, as the years went by the company also gained an increasingly bad reputation in San Francisco. Because it controlled all of San Francisco's supply of fresh water, it was vigorously criticized for being a monopoly. Citizens often complained of overcharging, and by the turn of the century it became commonly

Crystallized salt was collected in piles and transported to refineries for processing. This 1915 photo of the Leslie Salt facility in San Mateo shows the Hayward Park Railroad Stop (Leslie Station) near present-day B Street at 16th Avenue. A train can be seen at the right. Today the county's salt facility is located in Redwood City. The salt piles can be seen from Highway 101, and are a landmark for pilots flying into nearby San Carlos Airport. Courtesy, San Mateo County Historical Association Archives

known that San Francisco remained the only large city left in the United States to have its water supply owned by a private party. Therefore, in 1900, city voters passed a new charter allowing for the purchase of water resources. Residents also recognized that the growing city would soon need much more water than the peninsula reservoirs could provide. Some began dreaming of somehow tapping into the waters of the Sierras.

Meanwhile, the 1906 earthquake occurred. It did substantial damage to the holdings of the Spring Valley Water Company. The company continued in bad condition until 1908, when it was bought by William B. Bourn, who immediately began planning for its eventual sale to the city.

Bourn, a native of San Francisco, was born in 1875. He inherited the failing Empire Gold Mine and proved his entrepreneurial prowess by reviving its profitability. Later he invested in several local gas companies and then sold them to the emerging Pacific Gas and Electric Company for a substantial personal gain. With this money he was able to acquire the Spring Valley Water Company.

After the purchase of the company, Bourn decided to buy an addi-

Workmen pose in front of the wooden scaffold erected during construction of the Crystal Springs Dam in the late 1880s. At the time of its creation the dam, brainchild of Herman Schussler, was the largest concrete dam in the world. It withstood the 1906 earthquake with no detectable damage; had the dam broken, the city of San Mateo would have been flooded with 20 billion gallons of water. Courtesy, San Mateo County Historical Association Archives

tional 700 acres south of Upper Crystal Springs Lake for $90,000 in order to create an estate. He engaged architect Willis Polk to design his new home after the Irish Country Style with certain embellishments. Bourn called the place "Filoli," which is a combination of three words: fight, love, and live.

Bourn's desire to sell the Spring Valley Water Company evolved into a long and hard task. City planners had focused on the Hetch Hetchy Valley south of Yosemite as the location for a new dam. Here a lake could be formed, and, as needed, the water could be piped 150 miles across the Central Valley, through the Coast Range, and under San Francisco Bay to the reservoirs of San Mateo County. Of course this required the expenditure of a great amount of public money (eventually $120,000,000), and it also called for the flooding of the beautiful Hetch Hetchy Valley.

Hetch Hetchy lies in Yosemite National Park, and, when plans developed to forever change its appearance, conservationists, led by John Muir, came forward to oppose the project. A long political battle resulted that ended in 1913 when President Woodrow Wilson signed the Raker Act into law, enabling the project to begin.

Construction took 21 years and 89 lives. Meanwhile, Bourn's long-anticipated sale finally came about in 1930. The City of San Francisco purchased the 20,000 acres of the Spring Valley Water Company for $41,000,000. On October 24, 1934, water from the Sierras was allowed to stream into the Crystal Springs Reservoir for the first time. It flowed through the Pulgas Water Temple, which

The location of this Romanesque temple-like monument, known as the Pulgas Water Temple, is the point from which water piped from the Sierras empties into the Crystal Springs Reservoir. The temple is accessible to the public from Cañada Road, which parallels Interstate 280, and is the centerpiece of a garden-like area from which the reservoir system may be viewed. From San Francisco Public Utilities. Courtesy, San Mateo County Historical Archives

had been built to commemorate the occasion.

Thus San Francisco had successfully ended its quest for a reliable water supply. For San Mateo County the consequences also were great. The new 400-million-gallon-a-day capacity of the San Francisco Water Department also guaranteed a source of water for it. Additionally, a public body, charged with keeping the water clean and surrounding lands free of development, now owned much of the center of the county. Both of these factors had much to do with the way San Mateo County grew in the years that followed.

PATTERNS

OF GROWTH

THE SAN FRANCISCO-SAN JOSE RAILROAD

While the coast side never had a railroad completed through it, the bay side had a different story. Early on it was recognized that transportation between San Francisco, the state's most important city, and San Jose, the state's sometime capital, was important. During the 1850s, whether one traveled by boat or by stagecoach, the trip took a full day. The stage ride was preferred, but it was an uncomfortable and expensive ordeal ($35 round trip).

To answer the need for transportation between the cities, three peninsula residents—Charles Polhemus, Timothy Guy Phelps, and Peter Donahue—formed the San

Facing page: *Operational since the 1970s, the sleek electric trains of the BART transportation system travel above the street surface in northern San Mateo County. Daly City is the present terminus, but discussions continue regarding the extension of the system. Courtesy, Samuel C. Chandler History Collection, Daly City*

Francisco-San Jose Railroad Company in 1860. They enlisted local governmental support for the venture. The City and the County of San Francisco invested $200,000, as did Santa Clara County. San Mateo County made $100,000 available.

Unlike the men who worked on the Oceanshore Railroad, the builders of the San Francisco-San Jose did not have severe engineering difficulties. The route of this track did not call for the penetration of mountains, the fording of deep gullies, or construction on sheer cliffs hundreds of feet above the crashing ocean. The bay side's railroad followed the old mission road, long known as the flattest and least encumbered route south from San Francisco.

The Civil War interrupted the progress of the builders slightly. Still, track was laid as far south as Palo Alto by 1863, and the railroad was completed early in 1864. A commuter could now travel between San Francisco and San Jose in one

With the demise of stagecoach transportation, public vehicles were still needed to transport passengers from the bay side railroad line. This early twentieth century photo depicts one of the first omnibuses used in the southern county towns of Woodside and La Honda. Courtesy, San Mateo County Historical Association Archives

hour and 15 minutes. Twice daily the railroad had four or six passenger trains running the 40-mile route.

Phelps' original Southern Pacific Railroad absorbed the San Francisco-San Jose in 1868. The Central Pacific of the "Big Four" (Leland Stanford, Collis Huntington, Charles Crocker, and Mark Hopkins) in turn bought out this company in 1890. Despite the ownership changes, the people of the peninsula's bay side continuously had a dependable, convenient, speedy, and comfortable means of transportation.

One might ask why San Mateo County did not attract more residents during the nineteenth cen-

Above: *This was Simon Knight's stage, at the La Honda Hotel in 1888. Before the San Francisco-San Jose Railroad was built, the stagecoach was the major means of transportation in the area. Even after the completion of the railroad, stagecoach service continued to connect the towns on the coast side and in the coastal hills with the more populous bay side of San Mateo County. Stagecoach service continued well into the twentieth century. Courtesy, San Mateo County Historical Association Archives*

Left: *The completion of the San Francisco-San Jose railroad in 1864 made travel from San Francisco to San Mateo County significantly easier, and spurred residential growth on the peninsula. This photograph shows the railroad crossing San Francisquito Creek, the boundary between San Mateo County and Santa Clara County to the south. Courtesy, San Mateo County Historical Association Archives*

tury with this efficient railroad in place. In 1860 there were 5,300 people residing in the county. By 1900 there were 12,000. While the population more than doubled in 40 years, the county still grew far more slowly than any other in the Bay Area.

A real estate brochure of the 1890s, probably published by the Sharon Estate, pointed out the obvious advantages San Mateo County had over other counties: "Excepting none, San Mateo is much more accessible than any other place of suburban residence around San Francisco." It explained that in order to cross the bay to north and east bay communities, one had to catch a streetcar to the

ferry and then catch another streetcar or train to get home. To commute to the central peninsula, on the other hand, one merely needed to take a five-minute ride on the tramway from Market Street to the railroad station, and then in only 35 minutes one could be at a place like Burlingame.

Perhaps this very convenience retarded San Mateo County's growth. No one knew the peninsula's advantages better than the railroad barons and other members of San Francisco's elite. They bought up huge tracts of property to create their elegant estates. By purchasing much of the most accessible land, they may have prevented others from coming.

THE PLAYGROUND FOR SAN FRANCISCO'S ELITE

San Mateo County had more to offer San Francisco's elite than simply good transportation. The environment offered the best in suburban living and recreational pursuits. Climatically the peninsula was known as one of the most favorable locations in the nation, with mild temperatures all year long. In addition, the county remained quite rural, and this was a draw in itself. As late as 1890 only 10,000 people lived in the county. Excellent conditions existed for sportsmen. Deer abounded in the foothills, the marshlands teemed with game birds, and fishing in local creeks proved superb. On weekends bicyclists dotted the El Camino Real, one of the best roads in the state. The bathing beach at Coyote Point was one of the most popular in the Bay Area.

Besides all this, the character of the county represented something unique and appealing to San Francisco's upper classes. In the days when the British Empire was at the pinnacle of its power, Americans of higher social status tended to admire and emulate the English aristocracy. It seems that conditions were right for trying to capture that

way of life in San Mateo County. A turn of the century *Sunset Magazine* article explained:

There is not the least hazard in asserting that in no section of the United States—or in this hemisphere, in fact—[is there a place] where an Englishman of sporting proclivities would feel so much at home as in San Mateo County. This section is nearly a counterpart of the most favored parts of the mother country, saving that in place of baronial halls and castles, built centuries ago, there are palatial residences of later date.

Of all the social sets down the peninsula that attempted to bring the best of the old world to the new, none tried harder than the members of the Burlingame Country Club. *Sunset Magazine* pointed out:

Everything is decidedly English in Burlingame and its immediate neighborhood. Horses anglicized, drags, traps, harness saddles of English manufacture, the prevailing garb the handiwork of the best London tailors, and the graduates of Oxford and Cambridge are here to recount the glories, to tell the tales of college life

For almost a century Coyote Point has been a favorite spot for picnickers. This photo, taken in 1905, shows a group taking advantage of Coyote Point's rural, wooded setting. Today the area is more developed. Courtesy, Whipple Collection, San Mateo County Historical Association Archives

and pay glowing tribute, in the best English vernacular to these great Universities.

Club members participated in the sports of English society with particular intensity, and this meant plentiful use of the horse. At first they practiced horse racing. The club even attempted to copy the English hunt. On the surface this activity seemed simple enough. It required a pack of dogs and a band of merry riders to witness the outcome. One important component of the hunt was, of course, the fox, an animal rare in San Mateo County. It was determined that perhaps a coyote would serve the purpose. As it turned out, the coyote with its long legs and jumping ability was maybe too much of a challenge. Hunts reported to have started at the club went as far afield as the Ingleside area in San Francisco. It was with the game of polo that members of the club truly made their mark, frequently fielding teams of international importance in the years before World War I.

As in the case of the San Francisco-San Jose Railroad, one would have guessed that the great recreational attributes of San Mateo County would have acted to attract more residents. Instead they served to encourage yet further domination of the bay side by San Francisco's wealthier citizens, who created their estates as retreats for themselves. They gave little thought to subdividing properties and luring others to share the beautiful peninsula.

THE GREAT EARTHQUAKE

The seclusion of San Mateo County by San Francisco's elite was broken on the morning of April 18, 1906, when a horde of refugees began crossing the county line due to the great earthquake and the resulting terrible fire in San Francisco. There was also destruction in San Mateo County. The worst loss of life occurred in Half Moon Bay, where three people were killed when an adobe dwelling collapsed on those sleeping inside. In Redwood City most of the brick buildings experienced damage and the courthouse was completely wrecked. Estimates of the destruction exceeded

Following the example of the British, the wealthy class in San Mateo County adopted the game of polo. Played extensively and seriously at the Burlingame Country Club, the game required stamina, consummate horsemanship, excellent reflexes, and an expensive string of ponies. From the County Curriculum Department. Courtesy, San Mateo County Historical Association Archives

$500,000. Meanwhile, San Mateo witnessed substantial harm to its business district. Throughout the county, schools, banks, and saloons were closed, gas and electric power were rarely available, and local water supplies grew short due to severe pipe damage.

Still, the loss of property and life down the peninsula was light compared to the awful devastation in San Francisco. Many north county residents opened their doors to take in the homeless. In South San Francisco, the Western Meat Company donated food to feed the victims. As mentioned previously, for the north county the catastrophe in San Francisco fueled rapid growth, because many refugees remained there after their arrival. While the south county did not experience much change, the mid-county area also underwent expansion. This was especially true in Burlingame, where the mere name of the place served to attract those familiar with its reputation.

By the time of the next federal census, in 1910, the population of the county had risen from 12,000 to 20,600, a 72 percent increase from its 1900 level. In the next 10 years the trend continued. In 1920, 36,800 people lived there, a 79 percent aug-

The courthouse in Redwood City, seat of San Mateo County government, is pictured after the 1906 earthquake. Only the dome remained intact. The courthouse was later rebuilt, and in 1986 a complete renovation and restoration of the stained-glass dome was completed. Courtesy, San Mateo County Historical Association Archives

mentation from the decade before.

Still, while the percentage increases were impressive, San Mateo County did not keep pace with some of its neighbors in actual numbers, even though they were geographically further from San Francisco. For example, Santa Clara County, which had 60,000 residents in 1900, grew to 84,000 by 1910, and in 1920 had 100,000 living within its borders. Alameda County had a population of 130,000 in 1900 and filled out to 344,000 by 1920. Distant Contra Costa County expanded from 18,000 in 1900 to 54,000 in 1920.

The next few decades, however, had much more growth in store for San Mateo County.

THE AUTOMOBILE AND SAN MATEO COUNTY

Between 1920 and 1930, San Mateo County's population expanded by 110 percent: from 36,800 to 77,400. During the Depression years of the 1930s, although the rate of growth slowed to 44 percent, the county still showed a significant population increase to 111,800 by 1940. Over the 20-year period from 1920 to 1940, the county displayed a much more even pattern of development than that demonstrated after the earthquake. Almost every community on the bay side at least doubled in size.

The new popularity of the automobile sparked this surge in population. This new mode of transpor-

tation allowed many more people to consider lives in the suburbs, and a society based on commuting to work every day began to thrive down the peninsula.

The groundwork for this was laid much earlier. El Camino had its first portions paved in 1912 at San Bruno. Perhaps the greatest step was taken in 1913, when San Mateo County voters approved a $1,250,000 bond issue to create the northern portion of the Bayshore Highway. The state of California matched this amount.

Over the years San Mateo County remained a leader within the Bay Area in improving roads for automobile traffic. After World War I, as the cost of the automobile decreased in relation to personal income, San Mateo County reaped the rewards of its investment in paved roadways by receiving thousands of new residents who began to give many parts of the peninsula the character of a bedroom community.

WORLD WAR II

The three great events encouraging growth in San Mateo County were the Gold Rush of 1849, the 1906 earthquake, and the outbreak of World War II in 1941. Of these events, the last mentioned brought the most people and was the most responsible for the present appearance and character of the county.

Because this war had a Pacific theater requiring enormous logistical support, San Mateo County found itself in the midst of a national effort. Industrial and transportation facilities were either tremendously improved or brought to life for the first time. Thousands of job openings were created, attracting the county's first sizable numbers of black people and other minorities. Meanwhile the military constructed installations at Tanforan, Coyote Point, Half Moon Bay, and Montara. Tens of thousands of members of the armed forces traveled through San Mateo County en route to assignments elsewhere. Many remembered the place fondly and some returned to make it their home after the war. Of all the things that went with the war, however, the greatest development involved the substantial improvements to San Francisco Airport.

The county's aviation history had been a rich one before this time. As early as 1869, the first flight of a self-propelled dirigible had

taken place at Shellmound Park near today's Millbrae. Almost half a century later, in 1911, daredevil pilot Eugene Ely continued the county's aviation legacy at a Tanforan air show by being the first to successfully land an airplane on board a ship. Between the world wars the

San Mateo County, like most parts of the country, was active in the war effort. Here, Daly City residents pose with a collection of metal to be recycled for the military during the National Aluminum Drive of 1941. Courtesy, Samuel C. Chandler History Collection, Daly City

county became lined with airfields. In fact there were two in today's San Mateo: one at Bay Meadows and the other located at today's Parkside residential area.

In 1926 the City of San Francisco decided to establish an airport east of San Bruno. First called Mills Field and then San Francisco Airport, it began operations in 1927 and received a substantial boost in 1932 when United Airlines located there. During the years before the war, the airport was frequented by a variety of famous aviation personalities, including Charles Lindbergh, Amelia Earhart, and Howard Hughes.

Although San Francisco Airport already had some importance, it was not even the largest in the Bay Area until World War II. After the attack on Pearl Harbor, however, the United States government poured $10 million into it for improvements, enhancing it with several

16,000-foot runways and supporting equipment and structures. During the war, San Francisco Airport emerged as the most utilized air terminus in the Pacific Theater. When the war concluded, the airport's importance did not end. In 1946 nearly one tenth of all United States air passengers, more than 1,000,000 people, used the facility. It already employed some 6,000 people, and ranked as the peninsula's largest employer. By 1963 the number of people using what was now called San Francisco International Airport had jumped 10 times, making it the fifth busiest airport in the world. Maintaining its role as the peninsula's leading employer, with 30,000 people on its payrolls, San Francisco International Airport saw 15,000,000 passengers pass through the airport in 1975.

During the war and after, the mere presence of the airport was a boon for other enterprises. Maintenance yards, retail establishments, hotels, restaurants, and additional businesses sprang up to cater to travelers. Numerous companies came to San Mateo County specifically because of the convenience the airport offered for trade. Ranging from manufacturing firms to export and import operations, they all recognized that the peninsula had been transformed into one of the major crossroads of the world.

Other kinds of wartime industries arose in the county. South San Francisco, already known as the "Industrial City," was especially prominent as the site of increased activities. By 1943 Bethlehem and other steel makers employed more than 10,000 people. Meanwhile, some 48 ships were constructed, including

several escort aircraft carriers. One of the peninsula's pioneer electronics firms also started up in South San Francisco during World War II. EIMAC became one of the most important suppliers of transmitter tubes in the world during this period.

Other electronics firms receiving a boost from the war included Litton Industries of San Carlos, Dalmo Victor of Belmont, Ampex of San Carlos (and then Redwood City), and Varian of San Carlos. In the years immediately following the war, the electronics boom continued, and Lenkurt of San Carlos was born. It is likely that the development of the airport, the creation of wide freeways, and the availability of cheap land kept the electronics industry here in the expansive postwar years. Perhaps of greatest importance, however, was the presence of the two major universities in the Bay Area, Stanford University and the University of California at Berkeley, which had evolved into important centers of

technological research. Graduates of these schools proved to be incredibly valuable employees, pioneering the most exciting industries in the United States up to the present. As the years went by, the center of activity shifted south of the county line to what is now referred to as the Silicon Valley, but we should not forget that the technological revolution that continues to change the world we live in was, to a great extent, born in San Mateo County.

THE DEVELOPERS

By 1950 more than 235,000 people lived in San Mateo County, a 110 percent increase since 1940. The challenge to furnish homes for these people was, of course, substantial. The federal government provided some low cost housing. It completed projects in Millbrae, San Bruno, and South San Francisco. Immediately after the war, the private sector also became involved. Several individual developers came forward to provide homes, and reaped huge monetary rewards for doing so.

Henry Dolger was perhaps the prototypical developer for San Mateo County. He began his work here by building more than 3,000 housing units for defense workers in South San Francisco and other areas. In 1945 he purchased 1,300 acres west of Daly City and began creating the Westlake tracts. Over a 20-year period, homes for 20,000 people were constructed there. Westlake was annexed to Daly City in stages as the development progressed.

In a similar way Fred and Carl Gellert started by building houses contracted by the government. After the war they purchased one

Although it is named the San Francisco International Airport, this airfield, once Mills Field, is surrounded by San Mateo County. The airport was established by the City of San Francisco. This circa 1940 photograph shows the terminal as it was then, a far cry from the present-day multi-terminal international facility. Courtesy, San Mateo County Historical Association Archives

thousand acres known as the Serramonte subdivision. As it was completed it was also annexed to Daly
City.

Perhaps no other place in the
county was more affected by the
postwar activity than Daly City. Between 1950 and 1960 it grew from a
town of 15,000 to a city of 60,000.
Today Daly City, which has more
than 80,000 residents, rivals San Mateo as the largest city in the county.

While Daly City was certainly
the leader, development took place
everywhere. In San Mateo David
Bohannon created the Hillsdale
area. Bohannon had also been a
builder of wartime housing, but he
built outside of San Mateo County.
After the war he began working on
an idea he had before Pearl Harbor
was attacked: developing a garden-
like community of apartments and
single family houses with a shopping center. By 1953 some 500
apartments had been completed,
and by 1960 the shopping center
was in full operation with three big
department stores (Sears, Macy's,
and the Emporium) in place.

East of San Mateo, developer T.
Jack Foster, Sr., perhaps took the
greatest risks. His path to trans-
forming Brewer's Island into a city
of thousands of residents was an
amazing one.

Foster was born in 1902 in Texas.
After his mother and father died
when he was five years old, his
large family broke up. Despite this
rough start in life, Foster put himself through law school and, while
doing so, earned the distinction of
becoming the country's first student mayor by winning an election
in Norman, Oklahoma, in 1929. During World War II Foster led the effort to convince the Navy to establish an air station, air technical

*The postwar housing development that occurred in northern San Mateo County is illustrated in
this pair of photographs. In the first, taken before the war, the area west and south of the golf
course is undeveloped. The second photo, with the same golf course seen in the center, was
taken in the 1960s. The development of the Westlake area to the north and west of the course
and the Serramonte area to the south and west is clearly evident. Courtesy, Samuel C. Chandler
History Collection, Daly City*

training center, gunnery range, and hospital at Norman, which, of course, helped boost the local economy.

After the war he began building housing on southwestern military bases, notably Biggs Air Force Base in El Paso, Texas, and Fort Ord in California. He then involved himself in developing civilian housing in California, Texas, New Mexico, Kansas, and Hawaii. His exposure to northern California during his work at Fort Ord induced him to retire there in 1958.

This retirement lasted less than one year, because Foster decided to bring his three sons in on an ambitious new development in California. After an extensive search, they settled on Brewer's Island.

This acreage had once been San Mateo County bayline marshlands. However, in 1900, it was drained and diked and for many years was the site of the Frank M. Brewer Dairy Farm. The Fosters purchased it from the Leslie Salt Company for development in 1958. They were attracted to the site because of its large size and easy access to highways 101 and 92.

The Fosters called their future development a "planned community," because it took into account various engineering, architectural, and social concerns. The concept was based on similar projects in postwar England, where entire towns were pieced back together after the bombings.

The new community was designed to house 30,000 inhabitants by 1976. This called for the construction of 5,000 single family houses, 1,600 town houses, 4,400 units of apartments and condominiums, nine elementary schools, two junior high schools, one high school,

230 acres of parks, and 2,000 trees. In addition, 40 acres were set aside for "houses of worship." The plans were deemed so innovative that in 1963 they were placed on exhibit at the San Francisco Museum of Modern Art.

One of the beauties of the projected development was the creation of several attractive lagoons within the future city. These were conceived out of necessity. Originally the Army Corps of Engineers predicted that the entire island would need to be filled to heights of between 8 and 12 feet for insurance against flood and earthquake, giving rise to substantial drainage problems. The lagoons, however, proved to be a satisfactory and eye-pleasing solution to the engineering obstacles.

The Fosters also added to the appeal of the place by selecting Eichler, Duc and Ellison, and Kay Home architectural designs over those of their boxy suburban predecessors of the 1950s.

Despite the various favorable characteristics of the Fosters' plans, there were critics. *San Francisco Chronicle* columnist Herb Caen wrote:

We have this big developer, T. Jack Foster Jr. [sic], who has bought Brewer's Island down the Peninsula and plans to turn the 2,600 acre site into somthing called Foster City. Now there's a name to wing the heart of a poet. Foster City. Sounds like a company town in Eastern Pennsylvania.

There were more serious opponents as well. The most notable were the school districts of San Mateo County, which asserted that the development implied a huge cost to the schools and would tax their ability to provide adequate services.

Because of the innovative design and the apprehension of more than a few individuals about the ultimate success of the venture, the Fosters encountered difficulty in financing the project through private banking institutions. They therefore asked for help from State Senator Richard Dolwig and Assemblyman Carl Britschi, Jr., who introduced legislation to create a special improvement district. They succeeded in forming the Estero Municipal Improvement District in 1960. Support for the effort was found from both the San Mateo County Board of Supervisors and the city of San Mateo. It was generally felt that without this help the land would be "unusable." The Estero Act (SB51) ordered that a self-governing district directed by a three-member board be created. Appointments to the board were mostly determined by funds invested. Thus the Fosters retained control of the undertaking.

Soon came the day when the first units went up for sale. Prices ran from $21,950 to $40,000 for single family houses. The first 115 Kay homes were sold in two weeks. By 1964, 2,000 names were on waiting lists to buy new homes.

As predicted, the biggest obstacle for the young community was the provision of adequate public education. Despite the fact that the Fosters had planned for and set aside land for schools, problems developed because it was up to the San Mateo Elementary and San Mateo Union High School districts to build and staff the schools. Many secondary school students had to be bused to distant Capuchino High School in San Bruno. Meanwhile, the San Mateo Elementary School Board, one of the groups most critical of the Foster City project, had charge of creating schools for the younger children. Initially the residents of Foster City had no representation on the board.

After lengthy political squabbles, schools were finally built. Temporary structures initiated the Foster City Elementary School in 1966. In 1968 Audubon Elementary began operations, and in 1969 Bowditch Junior High School was completed. No high school was ever built.

While schools became the hottest issue of the 1960s in Foster City, other areas of conflict surfaced as well. In 1966 a citizens' group asked that they have representation on the Estero Board. They were offered the right to attend meetings, but no voting power. These residents felt this was not enough and brought the question to Sacramento, where changes to the Estero Board could be made. Senator Dolwig, chairman of the Rules Committee, placed the issue in the hands of the Committee on Governmental Efficiency, which the residents of Foster City recognized as "a graveyard for unpopular bills." A Community Association in Foster City threatened to place "For Sale" signs on every front lawn on the island unless some positive action was achieved.

Finally, on July 22, 1967, in Senator Dolwig's office, an agreement was pounded out. In November of that year, two residents would be elected as voting members of the board. In 1969 a third resident would take a seat on the board, one formerly filled though an appointment made by the San Mateo County Board of Supervisors. In 1971 the voting basis for selection of board members would be made entirely democratic.

Although this accord had been reached, it hardly checked the political fires of controversy. The proceedings of the board were marred by a series of squabbles. In one instance a board member was arrested for breaking a law when he made two 10-minute speeches on assessments.

By 1970 citizens were beginning to consider whether they wished the Board to continue to exist, whether they should allow annexation to San Mateo, or whether they should incorporate into a formal city. It seems few wanted the Estero Board to carry on. Meanwhile it was understood that the City of San Mateo hardly wanted to assume the $62-million debt left by the Estero District, which would have been part of the annexation process. Besides, Foster City residents began to have a sense of their own identity as pioneers of a new community. They did not like what they felt was the "patronizing attitude" of those across the slough. An election was then held in order to decide what to do. In a stand of almost unanimous proportions, 2,265 citizens (98 percent) voted for incorporation of a new city.

Still, all was not settled for the infant town. Controversies continued. In its first year of existence, Foster City had six city managers. In 1975 a newly elected City Council fired all five planning commission members and disbanded the Park and Recreation Committee. Council meetings in the early 1970s frequently lasted until three or four o'clock in the morning. As late as 1976 three of the five members of the City Council were recalled from office by the voters.

Despite the political unrest, Foster City grew substantially through the 1970s and today approaches be-

T. Jack Foster, Sr., is shown here in a 1963 photo, five years before his death. Foster was the driving force behind the development of Brewer's Island, previous site of a dairy farm, into mid-San Mateo County's most ambitious residential development. The land was purchased in 1958 and the first homes were ready for sale in 1964. Courtesy, **San Mateo Times**

ing the beautiful model city envisioned by T. Jack Foster, Sr.

LIMITS TO GROWTH
Developments such as Westlake, Hillsdale, Serramonte, and Foster City were responsible for another tremendous increase in San Mateo County's population. The decade of the 1950s saw the population grow to 445,000, an 89 percent increase. In the 1960s the rate of growth slowed somewhat to 25 percent, and the population numbered 556,000 by 1970. During the decade of the 1970s, however, growth leveled off, with a 4 percent increase to 580,000 in 1980.

The drop in the growth rate was due to the lack of space, and there arose an awareness that many of the environmental factors that made the peninsula such an attractive place to live were threatened

73

This 1964 aerial view of Foster City shows virtually complete land preparations, with lagoon construction in the center and a small number of houses built just west of the lagoons. The city of San Mateo is seen in the background; the oval track just left of center at the top is the Bay Meadows racetrack. Photo by Air Photo Company, Inc. Courtesy, **San Mateo Times**

by further population increases. Some of the initial clashes between developers and individuals now known as environmentalists focused on the county's bay lands.

Residents of the county could look back to the 1920s and the destruction of the oyster industry because of pollution as a signal that all was not well with the bay. Pollution of this great estuary was a regional matter, however, and

required the cooperation of all the town and county governments that lined the body of water. Not until 1947 did the situation become so uncontrolled that the State Board of Public Health refused to issue permits for disposal of untreated wastes throughout California. By 1959, $130 million had been spent on sewage systems around the bay. Still, San Mateo County was consistently listed as one of the worst

offenders against the environmental laws, at one point allowing seven times the legal limit of untreated waste products to enter the bay. Finally, in 1963, the San Francisco Bay Quality Control Board threatened to sue the county unless it met its responsibilities, which it did by joining the South Bay TriCounty Sewage Committee.

During the 1960s it was not so much invisible sewage that

absorbed the attention of many individuals in San Mateo County, but the fact that the marshlands and bay itself were disappearing. By 1964 some 188 square miles, or 60 percent of the marshlands of the San Francisco Bay, had been filled, along with another 53 square miles of bay itself. Newspaper columnists such as Harold Gilliam warned residents of the Bay Area that they should "cherish memories" of the estuary, for when it was gone the region would resemble the Los Angeles Basin.

There then developed a grass-roots movement to oppose the filling, and the citizens of the San Mateo County town of Brisbane fired

the community. San Francisco Mayor John Shelly explained, "You can't let the garbage lie in the streets." Dr. Paul Goerche, a Brisbane city councilman, responded by verbally attacking the "filler barons" and forming a committee called by a name characteristic of the language of the 1960s, "Garbage A-Go-Go."

This group joined with the powerful Save San Francisco Bay Association and others to force Governor "Pat" Brown to call a special session of the legislature in 1964. California politicians with 20 years and more of experience witnessed an unparalleled barrage of telephone calls and letters. One group

planned projects to be delayed because some citizens like to look at water?" The environmentalists made significant points, however, by describing the importance of the marshlands and bay to the ecology of the region. Some captains of industry sided with them. W.J. McClung of South San Francisco's Bethlehem Steel called the bay "a great natural asset." Others listed the economic benefits of conserving the bay for the tourist and recreational industries. One concluded, "It's not good business in the long run to destroy our natural resources." The hearings resulted in the creation of the San Francisco Bay Conservation and Development Commission, which immediately placed a moratorium on future filling operations on the bay line.

No longer could developers look to the marshlands as future sites for housing or business tracts. This left the county in a dilemma. The space for development on the bay side of the peninsula had been largely taken up. West of it were the hills of the San Francisco Water Department, protected as open space. As attention began to focus on the long-forgotten coast side, new state laws were enacted to preserve this portion of the county.

The situation remains such up to the present. Without space available to grow, real estate prices on the peninsula have rocketed upwards. Many who wish to make a life here cannot find a place to reside. Others, who do live here, are faced with having to leave because of the high cost of living. Many difficult choices will have to be made about growth in San Mateo County. It is perhaps the most pressing issue for the future.

Residents of Foster City were quick to take advantage of the recreation afforded by the lagoons located in the city. This 1979 photograph seemingly depicts a chaotic dinghy race in progress.
Courtesy, **San Mateo Times**

one of the first salvos of this campaign. Here local people became enraged when they discovered that the Sunset Scavenger Corporation had bought 250 acres of marshlands adjacent to their town for use as a garbage dump. Residents learned that for the next 25 years, Sunset intended to dispose of the City of San Francisco's daily 1,600 tons of solid waste—only blocks away from a residential portion of

of protestors adopted a television toothpaste commercial, and sent thousands of small sacks of sand with a message reading, "You will wonder where the water went if you fill the bay with sediment."

During the ensuing testimony, many spokesmen from San Mateo County came out against the environmentalists, labeling them a group of "drumbeating ladies and bird watchers." They asked, "Are all

6

THE ETHNIC EXPERIENCE

In the last chapter we discussed numbers of people and when they came to San Mateo County. In this section we will describe who they were.

Even the first people to come to the peninsula, the Ohlone Indians, originally came from somewhere else. Their ancestors had crossed the Bering Sea from Asia thousands of years ago. The Spanish arrived after the Indians. Then, with the American occupation and the Gold Rush, came a wide variety of people from every corner of the world.

EARLY FOREIGN-BORN PIONEERS

The American occupation of California and the sudden increase in population on the peninsula due to the Gold Rush did not indicate that this region was to be dominated by

Facing page: *At a local arts festival in San Mateo County, a young Japanese girl in traditional dress performs a dance from her Oriental heritage. Courtesy, San Mateo County Historical Association Archives*

the descendants of those who stepped off the *Mayflower* at Plymouth Rock. The United States was (and is) a country of immigrants, and its hegemony brought a wide spectrum of settlers to the peninsula. Moreover, the Gold Rush drew thousands of argonauts from around the world. The beauty, the pleasing environment, and the economic opportunities to be found in California became internationally known, and the makeup of the people who came to San Mateo County reflected the state's broad appeal.

By 1880 more than a third of the 8,700 people in the county had been born in Europe. They came from at least 15 different countries, but by far the largest group of European-born residents was the Irish. They had come early on in the 1850s, became well established on the peninsula by the 1860s, and, by the 1870s, had matured into one of the most influential groups in the county. In 1880 some 900 individuals, or more than 10 percent of the population of San Mateo County,

had been born in Ireland. Other European countries represented by sizable populations within the county's borders included the Germans with 341 individuals, the English with 202, the Scandinavians with 98, and the Scotch with 65.

The fact that more than a third of the county's population in 1880 was born in Europe does not take into account the large group of Chinese immigrants that lived here. More than 600 residents, or about 7 percent of the county's overall population, had come from China. As stated previously, many had come to the peninsula after the completion of the transcontinental railroad. They conducted the profitable shrimp fishing operations off the bay lands. They also provided much of the cheap labor necessary in the lumber camps and on farms. Most of these immigrants were young, single men from southern China, looking to make their fortunes in California and then return to their homeland. The percentage of Chinese residents never moved higher

than it stood in the early 1880s. This was due mostly to the Chinese Exclusion Law of 1882, which halted immigration from that Asian country. To a great extent immigrants from two other nations, Portugal and Italy, filled the vacuum for cheap labor.

THE PORTUGUESE

Actually, the first Portuguese settlers arrived in the 1860s. About 80 percent of these immigrants settled on the coast side. Most had been farmers or fishermen in the Azores. By 1890 the Portuguese population equalled about 500 souls, or 5 percent of the total population of San Mateo County.

Like the Chinese, the Portuguese became involved in a maritime industry with which they were very familiar in their native land. The California gray whales and humpback whales migrated annually off the coast, and the Portuguese were expert whalers. Unlike other types of whaling operations, the whaling done off San Mateo County and all up and down the California coast was accomplished without the use of ships. Small lateen-sailed longboats with crews of about seven men would be launched after a whale was spotted from the cliffs. A chase would ensue, and the harpooning would begin. The Portuguese referred to the California gray whales as "devil fish" because of their inclination to fight back and swamp the boats, particularly if a mother felt a calf was in danger.

Once killed, the whale was pulled to a shore station, where crews stripped the carcass of its blubber. The fat was boiled down in huge try-pots in order to produce a fine oil that was in great demand. An average of 30 barrels of oil could be ren-

In the latter part of the nineteenth century, Portuguese immigrants to San Mateo County took to the sea in longboats to harpoon the California gray and humpback whales, visible from the coast in their annual migrations from the Bering Sea to the warm waters off Mexico. Harpooning the whales was a dangerous and difficult endeavor, demanding skilled seamanship. Courtesy, San Francisco Maritime Museum

dered from a California gray. Fifty barrels could be secured from a humpback.

At least two whaling stations existed in San Mateo County, one at Pillar Point and the other at Pigeon Point. An observer named Colonel Albert S. Evans described the Pigeon Point station in 1869 as a cluster of "some dozen cottages, inhabited by the coast whalers and their families." Evans wrote that these Portuguese people were "a stout hardy looking race" who "work hard." Evans also remarked

on the smell of the place.

The whaling industry faded away at the turn of the century as the number of whales decreased and other products replaced whale oil and the enterprise's by-products. The Portuguese stayed on the coast and to this day help give that section its charm and character, especially during times of the year when special ethnic celebrations take place.

THE ITALIANS
Perhaps the first Italian to live in

San Mateo County was Leonetto Cipriani. Cipriani was born on the island of Corsica in 1812 to an aristocratic family. As a young man he became involved in Italy's quest for unification, but he tired of the struggle by 1850 and decided to find his fortune by joining the search for gold in California. With much cargo, including an entire prefabricated house, two servants, and two friends (Alessandro Garbi, an engineer, and Guiseppi Del Grande, a patriot), Cipriani left for California in late 1851. Just before

This whaling station was located off Pescadero in southern San Mateo County. Taken in the 1890s, this photograph illustrates the whaling industry of San Mateo County in its closing days. A decline in the whale population and the discovery of easier-obtained substitutes for whale oil contributed to the end of California's whaling industry. Courtesy, San Francisco Maritime Museum

Following the decline of whaling as a viable industry in San Mateo County, many Portuguese settlers turned to other pursuits. This early twentieth century photograph depicts the Pescadero Stable, operated by the Enos and Nunes families. Other Portuguese families turned to agriculture and service businesses. Courtesy, San Mateo County Historical Association Archives

he departed, Victor Emmanuel II, the king of Sardinia, appointed him the first Sardinian consul to California, a position of honor but without salary.

After Cipriani arrived in San Francisco, his work as consul put him in contact with other pioneer Italians who were working to improve the status of recently arrived fellow countrymen. In fact, with Nicola Larco and Domenico Ghirardelli, he eventually organized the Societa Italiana di Mutua Benificenza, a mutual aid society that created the first Italian American hospital in San Francisco. The

organization still exists. Its main charge is the operation of the Italian Cemetery in Colma.

While his office as consul was a prestigious one, Cipriani desired to accumulate wealth while in California. He therefore resigned his position and set out with his companion, Garbi, on a rather ill-fated cross-country cattle drive and "scientific" expedition. After returning from the adventure, he purchased acreage that had once been a part of the Pulgas Rancho from S.M. Mezes, a law partner of Cipriani's cousin, Ottavio Cipriani.

At this site in what is now Bel-

mont, Leonetto Cipriani built a fine home and landscaped it beautifully. Garbi came to live with him, and the two men were often to be found in the company of "society ladies" at a nearby hotel.

Between 1855 and 1860 Cipriani made several trips to Italy and participated in the long-awaited unification of that nation. In 1864 he was declared a count when his old political ally, Victor Emmanuel II, became king of Italy. After hearing of this honor, Cipriani sold his estate and returned to Italy.

Cipriani's experience as an aristocrat was, of course, completely

Skyline Boulevard, a scenic winding road built on the ridge of the coastal hills which divide San Mateo County into coastside and bayside, passes Castle Rock Park in southern San Mateo County. The area is frequented by backpackers and rock climbers, who practice on the rocks there before tackling the more ambitious peaks of the Sierra Nevada. The view shown here is to the southwest, toward the ocean, and shows the still wooded slope of the coastal range in southern San Mateo County. Photo by Lee Foster

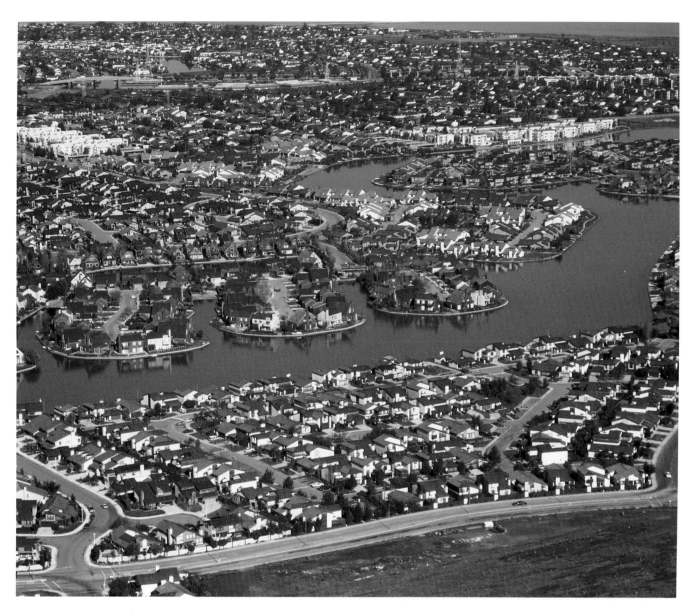

Above: *One of San Mateo County's most ambitious planned developments, Foster City features homes and apartments in parklike settings with lagoons meandering throughout. Photo by Mark Gibson*

Facing page: *A fishing trawler moored at Pillar Point Harbor in El Granada, just north of Half Moon Bay on the San Mateo coast, is pictured. San Mateo County had an active whaling industry for a short time in the nineteenth century, but commercial fishing activity is confined now to smaller catches. Photo by Mark Gibson*

Above: *Known for its produce, Half Moon Bay has, in recent years, also become known for its Pumpkin Festival, a weekend arts and crafts fair featuring food, entertainment, and a contest to determine the largest pumpkin grown. Over 100,000 people attend the festival, held in the fall of each year. Photo by Mark Gibson*

Facing page: *The shallow evaporating ponds of Leslie Salt create intriguing and colorful patterns when seen from the air. Travelers arriving in the San Francisco Bay area by plane can view these salt ponds on both the eastern and western sides of San Francisco Bay. Photo by Mark Gibson*

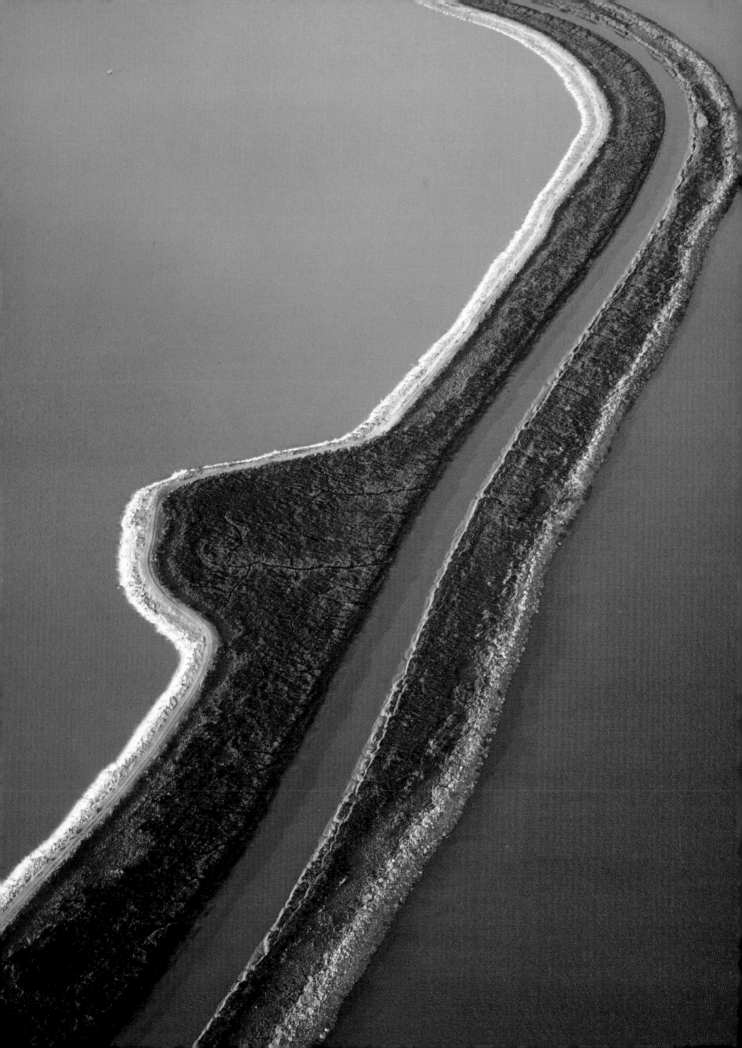

Above: *Many of San Mateo County's greatest mansions have been preserved, but not always as residences. Uplands, the second mansion of that name, was built in 1913 for Charles Templeton Crocker. Designed in the Beaux-Arts Classical style by architect Willis Polk, the building is now the site of the Crystal Springs-Uplands School in Hillsborough. Courtesy, San Mateo County Historical Association Archives*

Facing page: *The Mission-style Burlingame railroad station has recently undergone external renovation. It is located at the east end of Burlingame Avenue, on California Drive. Photo by Lee Foster*

Top: *Braving the icy waters of the San Mateo coastline (where the temperature is kept low by the close proximity of the Humboldt Current to the shoreline of San Mateo), these wet-suited skin divers off Pillar Point may be seeking abalone, a single-shelled mollusk which attaches itself to underwater rocks on the coast and is highly prized as a gourmet item. Photo by Mark Gibson*

Bottom: *This young elephant seal at Ano Nuevo State Park seems to view the cameraman with a somewhat wistful gaze. Since the creation of Ano Nuevo as a wildlife refuge and the protection of the breeding grounds of this indigenous coastal marine mammal, the elephant seal population has been increasing. Photo by Mark Gibson*

Above, left: *The yacht harbor sheltered by Coyote Point in the city of San Mateo is only one of several harbors for pleasure craft on San Mateo County's bayside. In Redwood City, where lumber ships and commercial travel once held sway, a number of harbors now cater to the needs of recreational sail and power vessels. Photo by Mark Gibson*

Above: *Visitors to California often regard the first artichoke served to them as a culinary practical joke! Originating in the Mediterranean, the artichoke was brought to California by Spanish settlers in the early nineteenth century. The cool fog and frost-free climate of the central California coast and the sandy soil of the coastal areas are ideal for the cultivation of this edible thistle. Artichokes are grown commercially in San Mateo County from Half Moon Bay southward. Photo by Mark Gibson*

Above, right: *A springtime view of coastal San Mateo County affords colorful views of indigenous plant life. Shown here is* **oxalis pilosa,** *a variation of sorrel, with clover-like leaves and bright yellow flowers. Further inland another variety of sorrel, with white or pink flowers, grows in the shade of giant redwoods. Photo by Mark Gibson*

The Tobin Clark Estate is one San Mateo County mansion that is still a private residence. Seen here is the home's elegant library. Courtesy, San Mateo County Historical Association Archives

The wood-frame construction and gingerbread latticework framing the gabled windows of Lathrop House are typical of many of the houses built along San Mateo's peninsula. Photo by Lee Foster

The Pigeon Point lighthouse warns vessels away from the treacherous rocks along the southern San Mateo County coast. The nighttime beacon not only marks the coastline, but the number of seconds it takes to complete a full turn can be measured by seagoing vessels to help them fix their

different from that of the Italian immigrants who followed. Like Cipriani, however, the first of these individuals came to California because of the Gold Rush. Most became discouraged and settled in the North Beach area of San Francisco. A few who had formerly been peasants came down the peninsula. Some took jobs as laborers on the farms of the Irish and German immigrants who preceded them. Others must have been struck by the apparent environmental similarities between their old country and the new. They purchased or leased land, and began growing vegetables the way their people had for generations.

The 1860 census reveals that some 13 Italians resided in San Mateo County. By 1870, however, the number leaped to 350, two thirds of whom lived in the north county. Most of these immigrants came from the region around Genoa in northern Italy. Almost always male, they were looking to make their fortunes and then return to their homeland and families.

Italians on the peninsula (and throughout California) achieved various economic and social milestones faster than their East Coast counterparts. This was due to two factors. First, the Italians on the peninsula came from the wealthier northern part of their country. They generally were better educated and had more money to begin with than did the Italians on the East Coast, where many immigrants came from southern Italy. Second, the fertile and inexpensive lands of California offered more opportunities to those who had been farmers than did the factories of the congested nineteenth-century

Below: *The Lagomarsino family typifies the Italian-American immigrants who succeeded in the farming industry in California. Shown here in a late nineteenth century photograph are family members and workers from the Lagomarsino's northern San Mateo County farm. Courtesy, Marsili Family Collection, Skyline Photo Graphics*

cities of the East.

The 1880 census shows that 442 Italians were present in San Mateo County. With the enactment of the Chinese exclusion laws in the 1880s, opportunities for Italian immigrants increased here at a time when people were leaving Italy in greater and greater numbers.

Gradually, poorer Italians came into the county. They worked as farm laborers, harvesting hay on the coast side and garnering potatoes in the north county. These immigrants still were mostly men, who desired to return home after earning a substantial amount of money. Many

Above: *Some early Italian settlers operated businesses in San Mateo County. This early twentieth century photograph shows the G.B. Pagano Store, one of the earliest Italian stores in Redwood City, and possibly all of San Mateo County. At left is Joe DeLucchi, with Tony Cassaretto at right. Courtesy, Redwood City Public Library*

Left: *Silvio and Rose Belli, shown here in the 1890s with their daughters Sylvia, Mary, and Adelina, bought a small store in Colma and expanded it, selling general merchandise, grain, and fuel. They also operated a saloon in the town. Though he retired from storekeeping in 1901, Silvio lived in Colma until his death in 1926. His wife and two of their daughters then moved to San Mateo. Courtesy, San Mateo County Historical Association Archives*

did go back, but others began sending for their relatives to settle here. As the years went by, whole families immigrated to the new land, drawn by favorable descriptions from relatives already living on the peninsula.

By 1900, 939 Italians resided here, and by 1920, 3,500 people in San Mateo County, almost 10 percent of the entire population, had been born in Italy. This figure does not, of course, include the hundreds of children born in California to immigrants.

After initially working on other people's properties, the ambitious new residents strove to work on their own lands. In the process, they transformed the landscape of the county. They grew spinach, cabbage, lettuce, cauliflower, brussels sprouts, and radishes. They also introduced garlic, broccoli, eggplants, zucchini, bell peppers, and artichokes. Due to their success, vegetables replaced other crops in the county, and, long before the outbreak of World War II, Italian Americans dominated the agricultural industry of the peninsula.

Besides vegetable farming, other early pursuits of Italians on the peninsula included flower growing and wine making. Many became involved in maintaining the gardens of the great estates.

Between 1900 and 1920, second- and even third-generation Italian Americans increasingly branched out into other businesses. They became particularly successful at operating small stores, hotels, and restaurants (some of which became notorious during the Prohibition years).

None was more accomplished than A.P. Giannini, the member of a Genovese family who established the Bank of Italy, later renamed the Bank of America. He married Clorinda Cuneo, the daughter of a coast side landowner, in 1892. They then settled in San Mateo, where they built a beautiful home named "Seven Oaks." As of the writing of this book, Giannini's daughter, Clare Hoffman, still lives there.

Giannini was interested in providing financial services to all Californians, even poor immigrant farmers. He took the time to travel to them, many times by horse. This approach contributed greatly to his

A.P. Giannini, founder of the Bank of Italy (later the Bank of America) and his wife, San Mateo coast sider Clorinda Cuneo, are seen here in a wedding photograph. Mr. and Mrs. Giannini built a home in the city of San Mateo and lived there throughout their lives. Courtesy, San Mateo County Historical Association Archives

success, since it led him to the creation of branch banking. Two of his first branches were located in South San Francisco and San Mateo. By 1940 his hard work had resulted in the development of the largest private banking company in the world.

While Italians such as Giannini continually upgraded the position of their people in peninsulan society, on the national level a quota was being placed on Italian immigration that revealed a certain prejudice against them. When World War II broke out, Italian Americans found themselves in the position of being even less popular due to Italy's stance as a nation at war with the United States. The hysteria of the period resulted in some actions against Italian Americans,

despite their overwhelming allegiance to this country. Laws were even created stating that those of Italian birth could not live west of Highway 1, because it was feared that they might signal offshore enemy submarines and planes.

Unlike the legislation that was directed against Japanese Americans, these ordinances were rescinded by the authorities after a few months.

JAPANESE AMERICANS

There exist many similarities and contrasts between the experiences of the Italians and the Japanese in San Mateo County. It is important to study the history of the Italians on the peninsula because of their large numbers and great successes. It is likewise important to review

Pictured are visitors to the Giannini home, Seven Oaks, in the city of San Mateo in the early to mid-twentieth century. While the young man and the children are not identified, it is possible that the girl in the foreground, wearing a large hat, may be Claire Giannini, daughter of A.P. Upon her mother's death, Claire returned to Seven Oaks with her husband and cared for her father until his death in 1949. Courtesy, San Mateo County Historical Association Archives

the story of the Japanese because of their accomplishments, but it is also imperative to acknowledge that of all of the peoples who came to the peninsula, none was consciously treated as badly as the Japanese Americans eventually were.

As was the case with the Italians, the first Japanese native to come to San Mateo County was a person of high social standing, and the place of the contact was Belmont. In 1872 Japanese ambassador Tomomi Iwakura, with 48 officials and 59 students (including five girls), visited William Ralston at his peninsula estate in order to finalize an agreement allowing Ralston to mint gold coins for the Japanese nation. Evidently the visitors were impressed with the area and with

Ralston, whom they referred to as "the Emperor of Belmont." After William Reid and his wife established the Belmont School for Boys in 1885, it developed into a popular school for young Japanese students sent to study western culture and science.

Sometime after 1885 poorer Japanese immigrants began arriving in San Mateo County. Like the Italians, this group was almost exclusively made up of men who desired to earn their fortunes and then return home. During the 1890s they mostly took jobs on the great estates, where they labored as servants and gardeners. After the turn of the century, they worked at the salt refineries, where they toiled 12 hours a day, six days a week, for 90 cents a day.

Early on, the new Japanese immigrants started up their own businesses. In San Mateo a bathhouse was established in 1891, a laundry in 1900, a tailor shop in 1901, and an oriental grocery store in 1906.

In town the Japanese were most successful with the laundry business. However, this enterprise became the target of organized discrimination. In 1908 white competitors formed the Anti-Japanese Laundry League in San Francisco. Their program on the peninsula included listing the white customers of the Japanese laundries and attempting to shame them out of being patrons. These efforts more or less failed. By 1941, there were nine Japanese laundries still in the county.

Part of the reason Japanese Americans were able to withstand the activities of both the Anti-Japanese Laundry League and the more widely based Anti-Japanese Peninsula League was that they had established social groups akin to the mutual aid societies of the European immigrants. The first gatherings were sponsored by Kenjin Kai or prefecture clubs derived from the old Ken or districts in Japan from which the immigrants originated. As in the case of the Italians, many of the Japanese newcomers in San Mateo County had come from the same province in their native country, and they encouraged yet other former neighbors to join them in the new land. Japanese Americans went as far as establishing a national organization, the Japanese Association of America, in 1900. The San Mateo County branch first met in San Mateo in 1906. Its annual picnic became the most important event of the year for this community. Beyond that, the association provided many programs for recently arrived immigrants. It offered information about American customs, employment, and housing. It also provided interpretation services, legal advice, and outright aid.

As with the Italians, most early Japanese residents in San Mateo County found that working on the land offered the best prospects. They discovered that their greatest monetary successes came with flower growing. Sometime after 1906, Japanese immigrants engaged in this enterprise in both the Colma and Redwood City areas. The endeavor became productive because of the work of Redwood City's Henry L. Goertzhain, who originated the utilization of cheesecloth for shade in the growing of chrysanthemums. Using this technique, great numbers of the flower were grown and sold. As the local market gradually became flooded, Sadakusu Enomoto of Redwood City began seeking out-of-state buyers and sent a shipment of chrysanthemums to New Orleans in 1915, during the All Saints Day festivities. The industry in San Mateo County expanded rapidly after that. Japanese Americans initiated new flower growing operations in Belmont and San Mateo. During the depressed 1930s, Japanese growers conducted various promotions in order to keep the industry lucrative, one of which was the creation of the popular Chrysanthemum Festival in Redwood City.

The impending Japanese Exclusion Act of 1924 represented one of the greatest problems facing Japanese Americans in the early twentieth century. Long before its enactment, Japanese residents were aware of its coming and its unavoidable implications. Most Japanese men still intended to return to Japan, but if they did not act, they would find themselves in the new land without any hope of having families here. Therefore a rash of "picture marriages" took place in the years before 1924. The man's family back in Japan arranged a marriage of this sort, using pictures of him to convince the families of eligible young women that a good prospective husband was available. Because the photographs were frequently years old, many a bride was surprised and, perhaps, disappointed, when her new husband greeted her upon her arrival.

This turn-of-the-century photo shows members of the San Mateo Japanese Club, possibly the earliest social organization of the Japanese community in San Mateo County. It was the forerunner of the Japanese Association of America's San Mateo chapter, which first met in 1906. The Japanese Association of America provided services to new immigrants to assist them in adjusting to the community. From the Ito Collection. Courtesy, San Mateo Times

The years 1910 through 1925 saw the development of the floral industry in San Mateo County. Many Japanese families grew flowers, particularly chrysanthemums, for commercial purposes. This 1910 photo depicts members of the Egashira and Eto families at a nursery in what is now the Beresford area of the city of San Mateo. From the Toshi Endo Collection. Courtesy, San Mateo Times

Nevertheless, a whole new generation of American-born children was brought into the world. They were called nisei by their parents, who were known as the issei. Some of the offspring were actually sent back to Japan for their education. Most were reared here, but they attended special Japanese "language schools" that taught the youngsters much about the lands and customs of their ancestors. Japanese parents felt that this was an important part of the nisei's education, because the issei still believed that one day the families would return to Japan. Between 1916 and 1930 language schools were formed in San Mateo, Pescadero, Belmont, and Redwood City.

Understandably there developed many differences between the first and second generations. The values of the old world were constantly threatened by the new American culture. The nisei even created their own national organization, the Japanese American Citizen's League (JACL). The San Mateo chapter was formed in 1935. The new organization specialized in social activities, and acted to inves-

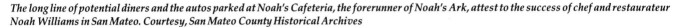

The long line of potential diners and the autos parked at Noah's Cafeteria, the forerunner of Noah's Ark, attest to the success of chef and restaurateur Noah Williams in San Mateo. Courtesy, San Mateo County Historical Archives

tigate discrimination in employment and other areas because of race.

The advent of World War II forever changed the JACL and the Japanese American people as a whole. As America's conflict with Japan became imminent, the San Mateo JACL placed a full-page newspaper testimonial to their loyalty to the United States in the *Burlingame Advance* on September 17, 1941. Unfortunately, the December 7 attack on Pearl Harbor by the Japanese Navy whipped up so much hysteria that the pronouncement was ignored. Immediately the Federal Bureau of Investigation rounded up issei leaders. Then, in early 1942, President Franklin D. Roosevelt issued Executive Order 9066, which gave local military authorities the power to intern Japanese Americans, regardless of whether they were citizens or not.

After being told they had but two weeks to sell all of their properties, some 1,200 San Mateo County Japanese Americans joined about 7,000 others at the Tanforan Race Track, which the Army had converted into an assembly center. After a four-month stay there, the group was taken to Camp Topaz, a relocation center in central Utah, where most waited out the war.

In the postwar period Japanese Americans returned to San Mateo County to once again become productive members of society. The shame and bitterness of the war years endure, however, and now make up a part of their unique ethnic identity.

MANY OTHERS

European, Chinese, and Japanese immigrants have had a substantial impact on the history of San Mateo County. Other groups, however, also deserve attention.

Black people have resided in the county from early on. One of the first to make a mark was Thomas Rolle, an ex-slave from Virginia who came to California in 1858. In 1873 he arrived in San Mateo County, and in 1875 he became associated with the "Star and Garter Road House" in today's San Bruno. The place was renamed "Uncle Tom's Cabin" as a reflection of its new management. Rolle lived at the roadhouse, which also was the area's post office. Facilities were present for eating, drinking, and an assortment of other activities. Rolle died in 1879.

Of all the blacks present in San Mateo County before World War II, none was more famous than restaurateur Noah Williams. Williams came from a long line of well-known chefs from the "Old South." He worked as a cook for the Southern Pacific Railroad until 1921, when he opened a restaurant on B Street in San Mateo.

The establishment became an immediate success. Motorists traveling up and down the state on the El Camino Real made stopping at "Noah's" a priority. It was said that Williams cooked more than 20 hams a day, and Sunday dinner at his restaurant meant waiting in line around the block until a table became available. In 1924 Williams decided to move to a bigger building on Third Avenue. He called the place "Noah's Ark" and decorated it appropriately with huge renderings of animals. Unfortunately the Depression of the 1930s put an end to the business.

Despite these beginnings, the real history of blacks (and many others) in San Mateo County began with the outbreak of World War II. The war industries drew thousands of poor southern blacks to the Bay Area. Many worked on the peninsula. In the immediate postwar period, a sizable number of blacks came to live in East Palo Alto. Regrettably the Bayshore Freeway tended to isolate the area. Whites moved out. Jobs became scarce, and, as was the case with Watts and other places in California, a sort of suburban ghetto was born.

During the 1960s East Palo Alto experienced various kinds of troubles characteristic of the racial unrest of the period. Ravenswood High School became the focus of some violence as school segregation developed into an important issue.

Recently East Palo Alto incorporated as a separate city. Many problems still exist, but a new leadership is taking shape that may prove equal to the challenge.

During the postwar period the entire county began experiencing substantial increases in its nonwhite populations. This was especially true in the 1960s. During that decade, as the white population increased at a 19 percent rate, the nonwhite population increased 153 percent. The Hispanics led all other groups in sheer numbers.

In 1960 about 4 percent, or 19,700, of the 445,000 people in San Mateo County were Hispanic. By 1970 Hispanic residents comprised 11 percent, or 63,000, of the total county population of 556,000. In 1980 Hispanics numbered about 100,000 out of the 580,000 people in the county, making them approximately 17 percent of all the residents in the county.

A look at school statistics reveals that this phenomenon can be ex-

pected to continue. During the 1979-1980 academic year, 39,854 out of 85,796 public school children, more than 46 percent, were nonwhite. This included 11,601 Hispanics (14 percent) and 7,722 blacks (9 percent).

The other groups represented within the 46 percent included Chinese and Japanese citizenry and some new communities as well.

Among those that have recently come are Polynesian people, particularly from the islands of Samoa and Tonga. This immigration also resulted because of World War II. During the 1940s the United States Navy built up its facilities on American Samoa, employing hundreds of native workers. When these operations were closed down in 1951,

many were allowed to find new jobs in California. Various churches sponsored further migrations from Samoa and Tonga in subsequent years.

By 1976 it was estimated that some 6,000 to 10,000 Polynesians lived in San Mateo County. The Samoans tended to settle in Daly City, South San Francisco, and San Bruno. The Tongans, meanwhile, moved into neighborhoods in San Mateo, Burlingame, San Bruno, East Palo Alto, and Redwood City.

Dr. Caroline Naufahu (recipient of the first Ph.D. awarded to a Tongan woman) has done a great deal of social work in San Mateo County that illustrates how there came to be such a large concentration of Polynesians here. She believes that

Above: Uprooted from his homeland and facing an unfamiliar, alien environment, this young Asian refugee touchingly demonstrates faith in his own future by pledging allegiance to his new country. Courtesy, **San Mateo Times**

Below: The large Hispanic population of San Mateo County celebrates its cultural heritage with such festivals as Cinco de Mayo (the Fifth of May, the day on which Mexico gained its independence from Spain). Here, in a 1987 photo, children of Hispanic heritage perform traditional dances in costume. Photo by Daniel Murphy. Courtesy, **San Mateo Times**

the Samoans and Tongans have appeared in the county for many of the same push-pull economic reasons that drew other immigrants. Additionally, she explains, "San Mateo is less urban than the big cities, and the climate, mild but sunny, is more like our own, so our people feel more comfortable here than in a more bustling high-powered environment."

Most Polynesians find employment at the airport. Interestingly, Dr. Naufahu reports that most of her people do not expect to stay in the United States. They plan to go back home when they have earned enough money and their children have their educations.

Unfortunately, many Polynesians have not found what they came to this country to receive. Making a life here has not been easy. Their native cultures are far less competitive, and this has led to some disadvantages. On the other hand, their belief in the extended family has offered much help, as have the Mormon and United Methodist churches.

The latest to arrive of all the new ethnic groups are the Southeast Asians from Vietnam and Cambodia. These people have come here as a direct result of the political unrest in their part of the world. By 1977 some 412 were present in the county. Most of them lived in East Palo Alto. A monk and former attorney, Dr. Nguyan Vannang has acted as a spokesman for these people. He cited severe language problems, unemployment, cultural differences, a sense of insecurity, and overall depression as the greatest problems for this initial group of refugees. Sadly, this original group was better educated than those who have followed, further handi-capping this population. In 1980 about 900 Southeast Asians lived in the county. Geographically, they have spread out more than the first Southeast Asians, with populations in San Mateo, Foster City, Redwood City, East Palo Alto, Menlo Park, and parts of the north county.

Of all the groups that have recently arrived, perhaps those coming in at the greatest rate are the Filipinos. In 1970 there were 5,676 Filipinos in San Mateo County, and they represented about 4 percent of California's total Filipino population of 138,859. The state's population of Filipinos increased dramatically during the 1970s, growing by 157 percent to the figure of 357,492. Nevertheless, the population increase in San Mateo County has surpassed this at 424 percent. In 1980, 24,053 Filipinos resided in San Mateo County. That year San Mateo County replaced San Joaquin County as the county with the state's sixth-largest Filipino population, and indications reveal further growth will become apparent in the next decade.

EPILOGUE

And so peoples ranging from the Ohlone to the Southeast Asian refugees have come to San Mateo County, and they have found all manner of challenges to contend with. They have had many different experiences, but they all have found a beautiful place with an excellent climate.

The past has shown that solutions to almost anything can be found. There exist, however, difficult questions for the future. Now more than ever, it seems that people must pull together in order to move forward. Problems pitting growth and financial expansion against environmental limitations will certainly represent issues for the future. The very diversity of the peninsula, one of its great charms, may prove to be its undoing.

The formation of the various communities and their rush to incorporate in order to maintain their identities has historically given character to the region. Each town has sought its own destiny. Still, there are topics such as growth that must be approached regionally, and the individual cities will have to act together. Likewise, all the ethnic groups (and we all have ethnic backgrounds) will need to recognize larger community problems and tolerate cultural differences. Together we will have to transcend geographic and ethnic differences, identify common goals, and work hard to achieve these goals if we are to maintain the traditionally superior quality of life on the peninsula.

CHAPTER

7

PARTNERS IN PROGRESS

Through much of its history, San Mateo has had the reputation of being a rough, unregulated county. Its early rural isolation and lack of government controls, combined with its location south of San Francisco, provided a unique climate for the founding and continued growth of many of San Mateo's businesses. More recently, San Mateo County has come into its own as a respectable, prosperous community with one of the highest per capita incomes in the country.

San Mateo initially provided a place for refuge and recreation where San Franciscans could "get away" with almost anything. Early sailors jumping ship in the 1830s hid in the county's redwood forests. During Prohibition rum-runners unloaded their wares in relative safety along the isolated coastline. Many recreational activities banned at one time or another in San Francisco were legal, or at least ignored, in San Mateo, and the county became a playland for San Franciscans. San Mateo's countryside was also a favorite place for family outings.

San Mateo became popular for home building. The completion of the Southern Pacific Railroad between San Francisco and San Jose in 1864 and the San Francisco earthquake of 1906 provided the impetus for the first waves of growth. San Mateo's early homes were the summer estates of San Francisco's wealthy families. After the turn of the century, more middle-class families moved down the peninsula.

World War II was the catalyst for the most dramatic growth of San Mateo's economy. War industries and then returning soldiers created a demand for new housing. Land was still cheap in San Mateo, and many of the old estates and farms made ideal sites for residential housing developments. San Mateo's increased population created a huge new market in which new businesses sprouted and established ones expanded.

San Mateo's wide-open spaces were ideal for agriculture and early industry, and San Francisco provided a large market for the county's products. Today its land is still relatively cheaper than in San Francisco, causing many new services and industries to move to San Mateo in search of affordable office space. The San Francisco International Airport, which attracts large national and multinational companies, has also been a draw for San Mateo's business growth.

Although its rate of growth has slowed considerably in recent years, San Mateo's economy has continued to expand. Once a largely agricultural, industrial, and residential community, San Mateo is attracting more service-oriented, white-collar businesses, although agricultural concerns still line the San Mateo coast. Changes in the economic climate have attracted new types of business. Economic and legal limitations have combined with environmental controls to regulate the county's commercial growth. Newer businesses have succeeded here because of their ability to fill a particular niche, focusing on specialized markets within the county.

The San Mateo County businesses whose stories are related on the following pages range from small family operations to large billion-dollar corporations. Their histories reflect the changes that have occurred in San Mateo County, and portray a continuing ability to adapt to and thrive in this environment. These institutions have chosen to support this important literary and civic project, additional evidence of their commitment to the profitable future of San Mateo County.

Facing page: Daly City was one of the first north county cities to incorporate. Through annexation of other areas it has become one of the two largest San Mateo County cities in terms of population. This is an early photograph of the Daly City Fire Department, circa 1925. Courtesy, San Mateo County Historical Association Archives

SAN MATEO COUNTY HISTORICAL ASSOCIATION

What started in 1935 as a public relations effort to promote tourism in San Mateo County has blossomed into the thriving and respected San Mateo County Historical Association. Founded with the help of the manager of the San Mateo County Chamber of Commerce, Roscoe Wyatt, the original purpose of the San Mateo Historical Association was to bring in visitors by promoting the historical character of San Mateo County.

The association soon expanded its role from promoting to preserving and restoring the history of the county under the leadership of Frank Stanger, a teacher at San Mateo Junior College. One of the most influential presidents of the association, he developed long-range goals that included the preservation of the county's historical sites and oral histories, and the acquisition of facilities in which to keep historical records and artifacts.

The association began realizing its goals almost immediately. In 1940 the group persuaded San Mateo County to buy the Woodside Store, a general store that was the center of the lumbering community in the mid-1800s. The historical association also obtained a room at the College of San Mateo for a museum in which to house its acquisitions, and that same year began publication of its journal, *La Peninsula.*

Stanger stepped down from the presidency in 1941 to become the museum's director. He continued to be a driving force until his death in 1980. He was responsible for introducing the theme interpretation approach to the museum's exhibits, emphasizing the relationships and continuity between events rather than just labeling and displaying artifacts.

Under Stanger's guidance the historical association also lent its influence to a number of successful preservation projects, which included convincing San Mateo County to buy the Sanchez Adobe, a historic residence in Pacifica, for restoration.

Stanger's replacement as director, Leslie O. Merrill, was also a skillful leader who contributed much to the expansion of the association's activities. During his first year as director in 1964, he doubled the county's funding and greatly increased the staff size. During his tenure the association also assisted with the formation of the Johnston House Foundation to preserve the James Johnston House in Half Moon Bay. Most significantly, the association's San Mateo County Historical Museum was accredited by the American Association of Museums in 1972.

After Proposition 13 passed in 1978, the historical association suffered lean times through the early 1980s. All the staff positions, including that of director, were reduced to volunteer status, and only through the work of these volunteers was the historical association kept in operation. Finally, in 1984, the budget was sufficiently strengthened to allow the association to hire a new director. Mitchell Postel was selected to fill the position and is the current director.

The San Mateo County Historical Association continues to fulfill its role as preserver and interpreter of the county's history. As well as operating three musuems—the San Mateo County Museum, the Woodside Store, and Sanchez Adobe—using volunteer docents, the association continues to publish *La Peninsula.* It also organizes various county historical events, such as the annual Victorian Days in the Park.

The interior of the San Mateo County Historical Museum. Artifacts indigenous to San Mateo County have been carefully preserved and are on display in the museum in a theme interpretation approach, which provides interest and continuity for the viewer.

SAN MATEO COUNTY ECONOMIC DEVELOPMENT ASSOCIATION

It was in 1911 that a group of leading citizens of San Mateo County gathered together to form an organization that became the basis for the development of activities and facilities destined to bring to the area new thoughts, new ideas, new people, and new businesses—the San Mateo County Economic Development Association.

An official organization was created at that time that had among its several objectives: "to unite and keep united the residents and taxpayers of San Mateo County for their material, social, and moral advancement, and to secure concerted action upon all questions of public concern."

Through the years other groups in various forms and capacities with many of the same objectives were organized as the county prospered. Chambers of commerce were established in the larger incorporated communities.

In the early 1950s a spirited group consisting of political and business leaders saw the "handwriting on the wall" indicating that the county was headed for a population boom and that renewed consideration had to be given to preparing for the immediate and long-term future of the area.

After many months and many

meetings the group assumed the name of the earlier organization and incorporated in 1953. Its first step was to bring a delegation of the Urban Land Institute to the area to study and recommend action for improving and controlling the overall development plans for the area.

Among the several recommendations made by the ULI group were that the cities and the county require some stringent changes in the direction of land-use planning, that a permanent organization be established that would consolidate county information under one roof, and that a program be established inviting select, suitable industry and business to the community. In 1955 permanent offices were open for the private, nonprofit corporation.

Its first major accomplishment was the development of a Business Climate Survey taken among those businesses already established in the area. This survey identified and addressed problems that required at-

tention as well as outlined positive aspects of the community, creating the tools for a sales campaign as well as a program anticipating the needs of incoming corporate and service-oriented companies. The association then set out to identify and establish San Mateo County in the national marketplace.

Through the years the organization's programs have had continuous and careful monitoring, keeping up with the changes that have taken place, most recently adding the word "Economic" to its name.

Its current programs are centered in five councils: The Properties Council addresses the problems of real estate; the Aviation Council works with issues related to the San Francisco International Airport and the two county-operated air facilities; the Growth Policy Council monitors the problems of land-use planning; the World Trade Council seeks to promote international trade and identify the county in the interna-

The San Mateo County Economic Development Association works to ensure San Mateo County's growth as a major residential and business center. Evidence of this can be seen in these photos of Redwood Shores 15 years ago (below) and today (right).

tional marketplace; and the Transportation Council works with the movement of goods and people in the county.

The efforts of the San Mateo County Economic Development Association continue to be channeled in mobilizing the mental, physical, and financial resources of the community to bring about orderly growth of the area's economy and environment.

LINCOLN PROPERTY COMPANY

Founded in 1965, Lincoln Property Company is a national leader in the development of commercial properties as well as the country's largest builder of multifamily residential real estate. Lincoln has developed more than 70 million square feet of commercial space and 140,000 apartment units at a cost of about $10 billion. Lincoln presently manages more than 35 million square feet of commercial property and 80,000 apartment units throughout the country.

The Western Region's Office Industrial Division has developed in excess of 25 million square feet of warehouse distribution, research and development, suburban office, and mixed-use projects at a cost of more than $1.5 billion, with 3 million square feet of office and light industrial space having been developed in San Mateo County alone.

Three major development projects account for most of this space: Lincoln Centre, Seaport Centre, and Willow Park; they cover very large parcels of land, a rare commodity in today's San Mateo County. Lincoln Centre consists of 400,000 square feet of light industrial and office space in Foster City. The first tenant in 1981, Applied Biosystems, Inc., is still the major tenant today. Seaport Centre, opened in 1985, includes one

Located in Foster City, Lincoln Centre consists of 400,000 square feet of light industrial and office space. Photography by Marvin Wax

million square feet of research and development facilities as well as office space in Redwood City. This park has a number of tenants in high-technology industries. The major tenant, Network Equipment Technologies, is one of the largest employers in the county. Other tenants include Gene Labs, Abekas Video Systems, and Devices for Vascular Intervention. Seaport Centre is the major research and development park in San

Mateo County and was the first park to provide such facilities locally. Willow Park consists of one million square feet of warehouse and light industrial space in Menlo Park. Originally the manufacturing facility for Hiller helicopters, the site was purchased by Lincoln in 1979 and, over time, the old buildings have been replaced with new, modern facilities.

Seaport Centre, a major Lincoln Property Company development in Redwood City, includes one million square feet of research and development facilities as well as office space. Photography by Steve Whittaker

DE MONET INDUSTRIES

Horatio Alger stories still come true, and the De Monet Industries story is one of them. De Monet Industries concentrates on the development, leasing, and management of commercial office space. In 1976 Joaquin De Monet founded this real estate company, the latest in a series of endeavors.

The entrepreneur did not have an easy start in life. He was born in Shanghai to German Jews who had fled from Nazi Germany. Then, after living in the Philippines for five years, he traveled across the Pacific Ocean with his mother and brother to arrive in San Francisco at the age of seven. After a childhood of relative poverty spent growing up literally in the streets, De Monet tried his hand at a diverse number of careers—from soldier to jazz musician to stockbroker. He eventually chose real estate development in which to make his fortune.

De Monet apparently made the right decision. In only 11 years De Monet Industries has developed

San Mateo Centre (right)

Century Centre I and II (below)

more than 1.5 million square feet of office space in the San Francisco Bay Area, Los Angeles, New Mexico, and Texas. In San Mateo County alone the company has developed approximately one million square feet.

The four office centers that make up its San Mateo County property are the Mills Court office building (in Burlingame), Century Plaza I (in Foster City), Century Centre, and San Mateo Centre (both in the city of San Mateo).

The Mills Court building was the first property acquired by De Monet Industries in 1976. At that time only one-fourth of this 50,000-square-foot facility was occupied. Within six months De Monet Industries was able to fill 98 percent of the building with tenants. The firm then set its sights outside of San Mateo County and proceeded to acquire office developments in Los Angeles, Albuquerque, and Dallas. All subsequent acquisitions and developments have been in San Mateo and Santa Clara counties, and De Monet has benefited from the recent migrating trend of large businesses out of San Francisco and into the surrounding communities.

The next San Mateo property that De Monet Industries acquired was Century Plaza I in Foster City. The firm purchased the partly constructed development in 1982. It completed the construction and was able to lease the entire facility in eight months.

The next project was a new step for De Monet Industries. Century Centre, at highways 92 and 101 in San Mateo, is a 284,000-square-foot office facility planned in two phases. The first phase was a six-story building finished in March 1985 that is now completely leased. The second phase was a 10-story building finished in September 1986 that is 90 percent leased.

In 1986 De Monet Industries completed Century Centre/San Jose, a 108,000-square-foot, eight-story office building located at the San Jose International Airport. Within six months of opening, the office tower was completely leased.

De Monet Industries' current project is its most extensive to date. San Mateo Centre, also near highways 92 and 101, is a large planned complex of a Ramada Inn and six office buildings totaling 546,000 square feet. Two three-story buildings were completed in December 1985; two more such structures will be available for occupancy in mid-1988.

De Monet Industries designs its office facilities to accommodate the requirements of its clients. The founder is personally involved in the design process, and has chosen distinctive architecture for his developments. He believes that these bold designs, which stand out above the surrounding landscape, reflect the strength and stability of the office tenants. De Monet Industries focuses on accomplishing these dramatic and functional designs economically. The company also contracts with landscaping firms to design landscapes that complement the buildings' architecture, and works with the individual tenants to develop interiors that meet their needs. Design details include luxuries such as athletic facilities, dramatic lobbies, landscaped balconies, and panoramic views.

These sumptuous, up-scale developments are designed for occupancy by *Fortune* 100 companies. Their nearness to the airport also makes these facilities convenient for national and multinational corporations. De Monet Industries leases its facilities to a number of large financial institutions such as Bank of America, Citicorp, and Dun & Bradstreet, and to government agencies such as the departments of Health, Education & Welfare, Housing & Urban Development, and Labor. It also leases to a number of other notable companies such as Prudential Insurance, Wang Laboratories, Phillips Petroleum, NCR, Nixdorf, Unisys, and Fujitsu.

Century Centre/San Jose

DAVID D. BOHANNON ORGANIZATION

A combination of foresight, hard work, and luck allowed Bohannon's company to survive and prosper through the lean years of the Great Depression. By the time the Depression was in full swing, sales were slowing, and Bohannon decided to change his approach to land sales. Rather than sell lots, he decided to build houses on the lots and sell finished homes.

One of Bohannon's early developments was Menlo Oaks, in eastern Menlo Park. Building began there in 1933 in the depth of the Depression. The advent in 1934 of FHA financing, which provided longer-term insured loans, greatly helped in bringing about the success of the project.

Hillsdale Shopping Center, 1987.

David D. Bohannon, founder of the David D. Bohannon Organization and the Bohannon Development Company.

The David D. Bohannon Organization, founded in 1928 by the man of the same name, has observed and participated in many dramatic changes that have taken place in San Mateo County over the past 60 years. This land development company has been continuously active in the growth and development of San Mateo County. Its activities have included subdivision lot sales, construction and sale of new homes, and development of the Bohannon Industrial Park and of the Hillsdale Shopping Center. In each of these Bohannon Organization developments there has been strong commitment and dedication to quality and to sound land planning.

The Bohannon Organization's earliest activities in San Mateo County occurred in 1928 and were confined to subdivision lot sales in the area of Menlo Park. Having almost no customers on the San Mateo Peninsula due to its small population, prospects for the purchase of the lots were driven by salesmen from San Francisco to Menlo Park. As San Francisco's population grew, demand for land south of San Francisco would soon follow.

In a broader sense though, the creation of FHA laid the foundation for a new growth industry—home building.

Bohannon worked in San Mateo County as well as with national groups in order to promote ideas for controlled and comprehensive land development. He became president of the Urban Land Institute, Washington, D.C., and with his executive vice-president, Ronald L. Campbell, a former San Mateo County planner, counseled city governments on the importance of planned growth for residential, industrial, and commercial developments through the study and survey of community needs. Bohannon was also the first president of the National Association of Homebuilders in 1941.

Over the years the Bohannon Organization would build many housing projects in San Mateo County. In 1935 land was acquired in the city of San Mateo, and homes were built and sold in the area known as San Mateo Park. By 1937 land had been acquired in Woodside for the luxury

Bohannon Industrial Park, 1981 (above).

A view of Bohannon Industrial Park with Atherton, Menlo Park, Stanford University, and a part of Redwood City in the background (left).

home subdivision of Woodside Hills. El Cerrito Manor, in San Mateo and Hillsborough, was constructed on the former St. Cyr Estate.

In 1939 the company acquired a portion of a former Spanish land grant, the 800-acre Murray Ranch, in the city of San Mateo, on which it developed the Hillsdale Subdivision. It was there that Bohannon first experimented with a precutting technique to reduce building costs. This method made it possible for him to accomplish major efficiencies in his war housing construction.

During World War II, Bohannon built more private war housing than any other developer in the country, although none of these homes were built in San Mateo County. After the war, however, Bohannon resumed his housing activities, completing projects begun earlier as well as starting new ones.

In 1948 the Bohannon Organization built the 700-unit Hillsdale Garden Apartment Complex. In 1978, through a joint venture with Paul Peterson's Whitecliff Homes, the Jennie Crocker Henderson Estate in Hillsborough was purchased and subdivided into 58 lots for luxury homes.

In Menlo Park, the Bohannon Organization had acquired land situated around the Bayshore Highway, which was to become the master-planned Bohannon Industrial Park. By the early 1950s Bohannon was able to attract companies of national repute to his new industrial park. Corporations such as Johnson & Johnson, Sterling Drug Company, Parke-Davis, Upjohn, and Raychem all located there. Today the Bohannon Industrial Park is still meeting the needs of the ever-changing high-tech industry of the 1980s.

Perhaps the Bohannon Organization's crowning achievement in San Mateo County, however, is yet another type of commercial development. Adjoining the Hillsdale Garden Apartments, Bohannon began construction of the Hillsdale Regional Shopping Center—now one of the largest employers in the city of San Mateo. An early tenant was Sears, Roebuck and Co., followed by Macy's and the Emporium. The center operated as an open-air mall for more than 25 years.

Bohannon Development Company was incorporated in 1969 to own and operate Hillsdale Shopping Center and other investment properties. David Bohannon's daughter, Frances Nelson, has been president of this company since 1975. Under Nelson's direction, Bohannon Development has continued to maintain, develop, and redevelop its properties. Hillsdale Shopping Center has nearly doubled in size, with the addition of a covered second story and Nordstrom and Mervyn's department stores in 1981 and 1982, respectively. The center is now 1.3 million square feet with 150 stores. The city of San Mateo received more than $2 million in sales tax revenues on sales related to the center in 1986.

David Bohannon remains president of the David D. Bohannon Organization, which continues to be active in real estate development. Three of his grandsons presently work for the company and are active in management, development, and redevelopment of company properties.

The David D. Bohannon Organization has also developed property in Santa Clara and Alameda counties, Lake Tahoe, Sacramento, Napa, and Palm Springs.

Bohannon's philosophies of land development are still evident in the present operation of the company. The David D. Bohannon Organization has always tried to anticipate and meet market demands for property development. It also continues to stress the importance of incorporating all aspects of residential, industrial, and commercial requirements into a comprehensive community development plan.

Menlo Place Office Park, Menlo Park.

FIRST AMERICAN TITLE INSURANCE COMPANY

When the San Mateo County Division of First American Title Insurance Company was originated, it was one of the first title companies in the country. George H. Rice, a former lumberman, started the firm in 1874. Having lost an arm in a lumbering accident, he served as San Mateo County Recorder from 1874 to 1878, and prepared abstracts of title as a sideline. The first offices of the company were in downtown Redwood City near the landmark Sequoia Hotel.

In 1908, after taking on C.M. Doxsee as a partner, Rice incorporated the business as the Geo. H. Rice Abstract Co., which prepared abstracts and issued certificates of title. Doxsee retained the business after Rice died in 1912, and the company remained in his family until recently.

Title firms in this country arose more than a century ago to address the common problem of land ownership conflicts. Due to the inaccuracies of early surveys and records, fraud and corruption were prevalent in land transfers. To determine land ownership and encumbrances, title companies prepared title reports by searching records, maps, and other documents.

The Geo. H. Rice Abstract Co. began issuing title insurance policies in addition to title searches in 1922. These title insurance policies protect the policy purchaser against title defects, liens, and encumbrances existing at the date of issuance. In the event of a challenge that questions the terms of a title policy, the firm provides legal defense for the policy-

The Redwood City First American Title Insurance Company houses the administrative staff, an escrow branch, and the division's Title Plant.

holder and pays valid claims or losses up to the amount of the policy. Soon after issuing title insurance, the firm reorganized as the San Mateo County Title Company in 1926.

In 1963 San Mateo County Title Company became an affiliate of the First American Title Insurance Company—also an old family firm founded in the late 1880s. First American operated as Orange County Title Company in Santa Ana, California, until it embarked on a corporate expansion program in 1957, changing its name to First American Title and Trust Company. The San Mateo County Title Company was First American's 10th affiliate under that program. First American now has branches across the United States and in Guam, Mexico, Puerto Rico, the Virgin Islands, and England. Title insurance and related services

have remained the company's principal business.

In the 1970s the San Mateo County Division modernized its facilities by computerizing its title records, making title searches easier and faster, and expanded and remodeled its offices. Although the modern facilities belie the early origins of the firm, its years of experience have produced one of the most complete and invaluable collections of property documents in the county.

The branch has insured a number of very large and unique properties in the county. It has had experience in insuring water-oriented sites such as Redwood Shores, a multiuse development in Redwood City, and Harbortown, a planned residential community in San Mateo. It also insured the title for San Mateo's Fashion Island, a large, enclosed shopping center, and provided the largest title insurance package in San Mateo County for the Fluor Mining and Metals headquarters building.

The San Mateo County Division of First American Title Insurance Company now has 133 employees. In addition to the division's Title Plant, the Redwood City office also houses its administrative staff and an escrow branch. There are seven additional escrow branches located throughout the county.

Named for one of the early partners in the firm, the Doxsee Building provides background for the staff of the San Mateo Title Company in this 1939 photo.

BOREL BANK & TRUST COMPANY

The president of Borel Bank & Trust Company, Harold A. Fick, likes to say that "Borel Bank has roots, not branches." That is, that bank's origins lie within the local community, and it exists for the purpose of serving that community. In fact, Borel Bank is the only bank headquartered in the city of San Mateo.

The institution was founded by brothers Harold A. Fick and Ronald G. Fick, and family member Miller Ream. Their family has a history in the banking business and has strong ties to the San Mateo community.

The first Borel bank was started in 1855 in San Francisco by Alfred Borel, a Swiss immigrant. He founded Alfred Borel & Company, a small commission merchant firm, and was joined by his brother, Antoine, a few years later. Alfred eventually returned to Switzerland, and Antoine, great-grandfather to the Ficks, took over the business. He diversified the firm's financial activities and continued to expand the company into a highly successful one until shortly before his death in 1915.

Borel was not only a banker, but also served as Northern California's vice-consul for Switzerland in 1868, and as consul general of Switzerland from 1885 to 1913. The Borel name became widely recognized and respected in San Francisco, as well as in San Mateo, where Borel lived from 1874.

The group decided to honor that name when it founded the Borel Bank & Trust Company in 1980. Both Fick brothers had had extensive experience in banking. Harold had been budget director for the Bank of California, and later opened Redwood Bank in 1970 in San Mateo. He managed that branch for the following seven years. Ronald had managed the trust department for the San Mateo branch of Wells Fargo Bank. Miller Ream had been a director of Redwood Bank.

When they made the decision to open a bank in San Mateo, they did so to fill a void in the community's banking services. They believed that the banking industry was becoming increasingly impersonal in a number of ways. The major banks were too large to give individualized service to their customers. These large institutions also relied more and more on bureaucracy to provide banking services, reducing contact between bank customers and bank personnel. The group wanted to bring something unique to banking by reinstating the traditional, personal banking relationship between the bank and its clients. They believed a one-unit bank, based in the community it served, could provide that service.

The bank incorporated in June 1979 and was financed by a successful public offering. The offering generated $3.5 million in capital and approximately 350 shareholders, allowing the bank to open for business on April 2, 1980. The bank opened its "world" headquarters in the Borel Square Shopping Center in San Mateo with 12 employees, all local residents.

Borel Bank was eventually able to build up a large volume of business, and to move into new, larger facilities in March 1987. The new location of the institution was an appropriate one—still on the site of the old Borel Estate. The Borel Estate was the San Mateo home of Antoine Borel. It was a familiar landmark in the area. Part of the old estate is now managed by the Borel Estate Company, of which Miller Ream is managing general partner, and Harold and Ronald Fick are limited partners. The present Borel Bank is now located on this site.

The Borel Bank & Trust Company's approach to banking has been successful. The institution has increased the number of employees to more than 50, and the number of shareholders to 500. Borel Bank & Trust Company enjoyed its highest earnings ever in 1986. It was also

The former home of Antoine Borel & Co., circa 1915. The facade of this building still stands at 440 Montgomery Street in San Francisco.

named one of 277 Star Performer Banks in the West by the California Research Report, a financial services industries research firm. Needless to say, the bank has no intention of changing its banking strategy. Its intention is to increase its local clientele, and to remain a one-unit bank. To retain familiarity with the local community, the bank's management consists of local residents, many of whom are San Mateo County natives.

Although the institution does not plan to open remote branches, it does offer services to customers who use the bank from outside the area. It is a member of two automated teller machine networks: the Instant Teller network and the Star System network. The bank provides its customers with a number of traditional banking services, such as checking and savings accounts, money market accounts, certificates of deposit, and IRA/Keogh accounts. It offers deposit pick-ups by special arrangement, business loans, and a full range of personal trust services.

The dramatic exterior of Borel Bank's headquarters.

BAY MEADOWS RACETRACK

Horse racing fans in California should be grateful William P. Kyne did not realize his boyhood dream of becoming a priest. Kyne, the founder of Bay Meadows Racetrack in San Mateo, is credited with "-bringing horse racing back to California."

Kyne developed an interest in horse racing in 1900 when he saw his first horse race at the Emeryville Racetrack. Although racing was banned in California in 1910, Kyne gained experience in bookmaking and other aspects of the sport in various states where racing was legal, such as Montana, Nevada, New York, Utah, and in Tijuana, Mexico.

Kyne ultimately wanted to bring racing back to California. With its great size and expected growth, California could derive huge tax revenues from a healthy racing industry.

That was exactly the premise on which Kyne based his 1932 campaign to legalize pari-mutuel wagering on horse racing. A pari-mutuel is a betting pool in which those betting on the horses finishing in the first

William P. Kyne brought horse racing back to California when he opened Bay Meadows Racetrack in 1934.

three places share the total amount bet minus a percentage for the track. By this time horse racing was legal in California under the "options" system. Spectators would actually buy and sell options on the racing horses that would rise or drop in value depending on the horses' performance. But this system was not immensely popular, and California only had one operating track. Kyne argued that legalizing pari-mutuel wagering would raise large tax revenues for the state. After a lengthy

and arduous campaign, Proposition Five passed in June 1933, legalizing pari-mutuel wagering, and providing for the organization of the California Horse Racing Board.

William P. Kyne opened Bay Meadows Racetrack on November 3, 1934. The track was immediately successful, and averaged nearly $100,000 in daily wagers.

Bay Meadows introduced a number of firsts. It was the first track in California to use a totalizer, "tote," a type of adding machine for pari-mutuel wagering. It was also the first California track to use the photofinish camera, and the first track in the country to use the electric starting gate. The electric starting gate is opened by a button in the starter's hand, and its implementation eliminated post delays and uneven starts.

During this time Bay Meadows also began the annual tradition of holding the Children's Hospital Day Sweepstakes. Starting in 1937 the track annually dedicated a portion of the day's earnings to the San Francisco Children's Hospital's building fund.

With the United States' entrance into World War II, all tracks were ordered closed to conserve resources for the war effort. But Kyne was able to negotiate for Bay Meadows to remain open under a number of restrictions. Among those was the stipulation that it donate its profits to the war effort. By agreeing to this arrangement, Bay Meadows was the only track in the state to remain open during the war, and it raised more than $4 million for government coffers.

After the war Kyne introduced quarter horse racing to Bay Meadows and a few years later assisted in the opening of the first quarter horse track in the country near Long Beach. Quarter horses were the horses originally used for racing and were trained to run the quarter-mile. But they were eventually replaced by the larger, longer-distance thoroughbreds. Quarter horses became popular again during this reintroduction, and they still race every

Jockey champion Russell Baze, the most consistent winner at Bay Meadows and the only jockey in the area to earn purses of more than $4 million, brings another winner home.

spring at Bay Meadows.

Kyne remained involved in horse racing until his death in 1956. At that time his wife, Dorothy, took the helm and served as president and general manager of Bay Meadows for the next few years. She turned the position over to Joseph Cohen in 1959.

Cohen added an important development to Bay Meadows facilities. He built a training track in 1960 that allowed the horses to train uninterrupted while the main track was being maintained. Cohen also added a nine-hole golf course to the infield, which is open to the public year-round, except on racing days. In 1969 Cohen retired, and Bob Gunderson replaced him as general manager, becoming president in 1973.

Gunderson added more improvements to the track. He built the Longden Turf Course in 1978, named after Johnny Longden, the record-holding former jockey and Bay Meadows trainer. A tunnel to the infield was also added, opening the beautiful Infield Park and children's playground. Gunderson also established the El Camino Real Derby, the West's premier stepping-stone to the Triple Crown. In 1972 he began the tradition of Ascot Day, modeled after the traditional Royal Ascot race meeting in England.

A recent dramatic change in racing also took place as a result of Gunderson's efforts. He and Rodney Fraser, vice-president of Bay Meadows, promoted a bill sponsored by State Senator Ken Maddy to legalize inter-track betting. Passed in 1985, this bill allows racing fans to place bets on Bay Meadows races from

Rain or shine, excitement mounts at Bay Meadows as horses and jockeys race for another spectacular finish.

fairgrounds and race tracks elsewhere in the state. Bay Meadows serves as the host track and beams the races by satellite to more than 10 sites in California and others in Nevada. This new development has reduced Bay Meadows' on-track attendance somewhat, thus easing parking and traffic problems. However, the broadened market for racing has increased overall revenues due to its greater accessibility to a larger segment of the public.

Horse racing continues to be a popular and lucrative spectator sport for Bay Meadows. The track now employs more than 600 employees and stables in excess of 1,500 racing horses, more than 300 of them year-round. Outside of the San Francisco Airport, Bay Mead-

ows is the largest taxpayer in the county, greatly surpassing the revenues Kyne predicted in 1932. In 1987 racing in California provided more than 150 million tax dollars to the state. Bay Meadows Racetrack has hosted a number of famous jockeys and thoroughbreds over the years. Jockeys such as Johnny Longden, Bill Shoemaker, Steve Cauthen, Laffit Pincay, Jr., Russell Baze, Fernando Toro, Marco Castaneda, Gary Stevens, Eddie Delahoussaye, Pat Day, Chris McCarron, Lester Piggott, Yves Saint-Martin, Pat Eddery, and Walter Swinburn have ridden there.

Some of the champion horses that have raced at Bay Meadows include Gate Dancer, winner of Preakness and the Super Derby; Determine, Kentucky Derby winner; Majestic Prince, winner at the Kentucky Derby and the Preakness; and Citation, Triple Crown winner. Great champions Snow Chief, Tank's Prospect, Lady's Secret, Super Moment, John Henry, Wild Again, Skywalker, Round Table, Alphabatim, The Bart, Interco, Native Diver, Sea Biscuit, Hopeful Word, and Judge Angelucci have also thrilled Bay Area racing fans at Bay Meadows Racetrack.

The Bay Meadows Clubhouse, with its historic art-deco splendor, is a popular dining spot for racing enthusiasts, and the Turf Club provides a protected, comfortable viewing area.

PACIFIC GAS AND ELECTRIC COMPANY

The early years of the twentieth century were a time of tremendous optimism and innovation. Inventors and entrepreneurs were using the newfound power of electricity to run everything. Electric boot polishers, horse clippers, and cream separators—these were just a few of the "modern conveniences" found on the San Mateo estate of Walter Hobart during the period.

Entrepreneurs provided the electricity, too. Hundreds of local light and power companies competed with each other in Northern and Central California. The Peninsula Lighting Company, Redwood City Electric Company, San Mateo Electric Company, and San Mateo Gas Light Company—all founded in the 1890s—supplied energy to Burlingame, San Mateo, Belmont, Redwood City, and neighboring communities. It wasn't a very stable situation. Small utilities such as these routinely engaged in rate wars and raced each other in stringing wire and laying pipe—sometimes down opposite sides of the street—to win customers.

Prince Andre Poniatowski, a Frenchman, was instrumental in binding the local utilities of San Mateo County into an entity that eventually became part of PG&E. Poniatowski had come to the United States in the 1890s to invest in mining. To supply power to his mines,

An early PG&E substation in Redwood City, shown here in April 1922. Courtesy, Pacific Gas & Electric Company History Collection

he built the Electra hydroelectric powerhouse on the Mokelumne River, using the old gold miners' canals to gather the water. When completed, Electra's five generators had a total capacity of 10,000 kilowatts—more than the mines of the Mother Lode could use.

So the prince sought other customers, including the cities of Oakland, San Jose, and San Francisco. He ran his transmission lines around the southern end of the Bay and up the Peninsula, and that put him in competition with the local utilities of San Mateo County.

By January 2, 1900, Poniatowski and his brother-in-law, W.H. Crocker, had incorporated the Consolidated Light and Power Company and merged the local San Mateo electric and gas utilities into a single organization. Consolidated was in turn merged in 1902 with United Gas and Electric Company, which represented Crocker's holdings in San Jose. Three years later United and several other large light and power companies were joined to form Pacific Gas and Electric Company, incorporated in 1905. That same PG&E serves this area today.

Other local power companies in Half Moon Bay and South San Francisco were joined in Great Western Power Company, which merged with PG&E in 1930. PG&E was, and still is, an innovator. By 1922 PG&E's hydroelectric system—including Prince Poniatowski's Electra Powerhouse—made California the nation's leader in hydro, surpassing even New York State and its Niagara system.

In 1928 the company brought nat-

The San Mateo office of PG&E in 1922. Courtesy, Pacific Gas and Electric Company History Collection

ural gas in from the Kettleman Hills oil field, quickly replacing manufactured gas from coal. Today PG&E's pipelines from Canada and the southwestern United States are a valuable asset among California's energy resources.

In 1954, to meet the postwar boom in the state, PG&E built Pittsburg Power Plant, then the largest fossil-fuel generating station west of the Mississippi. Three years later, working with General Electric, PG&E built Vallecitos, the first privately financed nuclear reactor in the United States. Today the company operates Diablo Canyon, whose performance has exceeded other units of its type and won for

Two of PG&E's many San Mateo County substations are located in Redwood City (photo circa 1936) and in the city of San Mateo. Courtesy, Pacific Gas & Electric Company's History Collection

it the Institute for Nuclear Power Operation's highest rating.

And, in 1960, the nation's first geothermal power plant was started by PG&E at The Geysers. Nineteen units are now in operation there. PG&E's recent experiments with solar power, wind turbines, and fuel cells round out its diverse generating resources.

Now time has come full circle, and once more the electric and gas business is becoming competitive. PG&E is changing to meet this competition by aggressively marketing gas and electricity, stressing the company's superior service and reliability, reducing prices to be competitive, cutting costs, and seeking new markets. This strategy builds on the historic strength of the firm and at the same time points PG&E in new directions. It retains the company's traditional focus on customer service, while unleashing a more competitive and entrepreneurial spirit.

The forerunners of PG&E were the strongest and most successful of the many entrepreneurs who sought to serve the emerging gas and electric markets in California in the past century. Since its incorporation in 1905 PG&E has dammed rivers, strung wires, and run gas pipe through some of the most rugged country in the United States.

After World War II, when hydro power was not enough to meet the insatiable demands of California for energy, the company launched an all-out fossil generation building program that successfully fueled the region's phenomenal postwar growth. When fossil fuel shortages threatened, PG&E successfully diversified into geothermal, nuclear, wind, and other alternative energy sources, and pioneered many conservation and load management programs to maintain the supply of energy to its customers.

Throughout its history PG&E has stayed on the cutting edge of technological innovation to meet its ideal of reliable, low-cost service. PG&E is committed to maintaining the company's record of evolving to meet customer needs.

BURLINGAME BANK & TRUST CO.

Burlingame Bank & Trust Co. is a newcomer to the county, but it already has a strong sense of its place in the community. It is a very specialized bank, designed by its founders to serve a specific clientele.

The bank was the idea of a group of local business people who recognized in the early 1980s that a successful bank could not be all things to all people. At that time, deregulation in the financial world had thrown many banks off-balance. Suddenly their markets were full of aggressive new competitors and they struggled to respond.

The Burlingame Bank & Trust Co. founders saw an excellent opportunity to fill a particular niche. They knew that personal financial services to small and mid-size local businesses and to affluent professionals and individuals in the community were being overlooked.

Most banks ignored small and mid-size businesses, focusing instead on large corporations or on products to sell to masses of consumers. Business owners, professionals, and individuals with busy schedules

and sophisticated needs were often lost in the crowd.

As the bank was being organized, a clear definition of Burlingame Bank personal service evolved. The bank would return to the old-fashioned values of banking where every client's name would be known by every employee. Every client would have an account officer, and at least two other staff members familiar with the client's relationship. For loan requests or deposit questions, all clients would have direct access to the bank's decision-makers. Consequently, the bank would be able to approve loans or arrange special services quickly and flexibly.

In March 1985, after two years of planning, Burlingame Bank & Trust Co. opened its doors, amidst marching bands and ribbon-cutting festivities.

New visitors to the office are treated to a whole new banking atmosphere. The interior reflects the bank's philosophy of personal service. All account officers and the president, Jeff Gardiner, have their offices on the main floor where they

are accessible to clients. The teller "windows" are actually individual desks with chairs for clients, separated by short walls and planters. Although the regular business hours are from 10 a.m. to 4 p.m., the bank opens before or after hours for any of its clients. It provides scheduled and on-call courier service, its own wire room, and the tellers even sell postage stamps for their clients' convenience.

The bank is committed to hiring and retaining an experienced staff, most of whom worked in major banks during their careers. They are chosen for both their banking skills and for their strong desire to place client needs first.

Burlingame Bank & Trust Co. is locally owned by its directors, founders, and other shareholders. It provides its traditional style of personal, relationship banking to clients from South San Francisco to Palo Alto.

The bank's interior reflects its philosophy of personal service to clients.

CAMSCO PRODUCE COMPANY

The main ingredient in Campbell's cream of mushroom soup comes fresh from one of the eight mushroom farms of Camsco Produce Company, a subsidiary of Campbell's Soup Company. One of those farms is on the Pacific Coast in San Mateo, just south of Pescadero. Here, by Gazos Creek, on the site of an old Mexican rancho, Camsco Produce Company's most successful mushroom farm produces about 16 million pounds of mushrooms annually.

The Pacific Mushroom Farm, Camsco's second, began operations in 1957. The farm had 40 mushroom houses and 50 employees, who lived in barracks on the farm. In its first year the venture yielded a crop of 603,154 pounds—two pounds of mushrooms per square foot. When the operation first started, mushroom growing was considered an "art," and few people were familiar with all the details necessary for growing high volumes of quality mushrooms. However, with increased experience and fine tuning of the growing process, Camsco was able to increase yield at its Pacific farm to today's rate of 5.5 to seven pounds per square foot.

The basic steps of mushroom growing haven't changed much since the farm first began. Although later Camsco operations have been built with more modern, high-tech equipment, none have been able to produce the volume that this farm does with its relatively old-fashioned facilities. Unlike most agricultural crops, mushrooms require coolness for maximum growth. Half Moon

Camsco's second mushroom farm was built in 1957 in Pescadero overlooking the Pacific Ocean.

Bay provides an ideal climate, making the farm's work much easier. No air-conditioning is required, and the consistent fog helps keep the mushroom beds moist.

Mushroom growing is a three-month cycle from start to finish. Mushrooms grow in a mixture of horse manure, chicken litter, cottonseed meal, and gypsum. Camsco gets the horse manure from racetracks around the state, thus performing a service for the tracks as well. The ingredients are formed into compost "ricks" and mixed, watered, and rested according to a strict schedule. This process allows the ricks to "cook" into the correct combination of organic components. The ricks are filled into growing beds in the mushroom houses—where the temperature, humidity,

Camsco's Pacific Mushroom Farm is still the most productive of its eight mushroom farms today due to its cool, damp coastal climate.

and oxygen supply are carefully regulated to clear the compost of ammonia. The mushroom spawn are placed in the prepared beds, covered with plastic, and incubated for two weeks. After about 23 more days of watering and temperature regulation, the mushrooms are ready to be harvested.

Camsco Produce Company entered the fresh market in 1979, and the majority of the mushrooms harvested and packaged go to chain supermarkets in California. The remainder go to Campbell's processing plants to be added to many of its soups, sauces, and other processed foods. A direct-store delivery service, started in 1986, delivers fresh mushrooms directly to stores in Santa Cruz, Monterey, San Francisco, and San Jose the same day they are picked.

Today Camsco Produce's Pacific Mushroom Farm has approximately 96 mushroom houses and 330 employees. Since 1982 the employees no longer live on site.

In the near future Camsco Produce Company plans to expand its direct-store deliveries of produce, which have been well received. While continuing its mushroom farming, Camsco also plans to branch out into other types of produce.

AMPEX CORPORATION

Ampex technology touches the lives of most Americans daily. When we watch television, or if we own VCRs, we are dependent on technology developed by Ampex. Ampex Corporation designs and manufactures products that record, store, and display data and images such as those seen on a television screen or stored on a video cassette.

The company was founded in 1944 in San Carlos by Russian immigrant and electrical engineer Alexander M. Poniatoff. He created the name Ampex by combining his initials with "ex" for excellence. The firm's first products were airborne radar motors and generators developed for the U.S. Navy.

After World War II Ampex developed the first American audio tape recorder, the Ampex Model 200. The company was backed by Bing Crosby, who was enthusiastic about the possibility of taping and editing radio programs for later broadcast. He became an Ampex distributor in 1948, and sold the recorder to radio stations, networks, and recording studios.

This product was the first of many firsts for Ampex. In 1956 the company introduced a revolutionary product that changed television dramatically: the first commercial videotape recorder. Before the advent of the commercial videotape recorder, almost all television programs were broadcast live. At that time recording engineers used film devices, called kinescopes, to record programs. The kinescope was aimed at a video monitor to create a film copy of the television event. The difficulty and expense of producing recordings of acceptable quality was often prohibitive.

The videotape enabled pictures to be captured on magnetic film as they occurred. The images were much cleaner, and the tapes could be used repeatedly and stored for long periods of time.

In 1957 Ampex was given its first Emmy Award for this technological breakthrough. The videotape recorder virtually ended live television broadcasts. Today 85 percent of television programs are prerecorded using this technology.

To edit videotapes Ampex developed, in 1961, the electronic video-

Alexander M. Poniatoff, founder of Ampex, with the first commercial videotape recorder.

tape editor, the Ampex Editec. Before this time tape editing had to be done by actual hand cutting and splicing. With the Editec, editing could be done electronically, increasing precision and reducing the amount of tape lost in the editing process.

That same year Ampex also introduced the first commercial helical scan videotape recorder. This type of recorder allowed images to be recorded on narrower tape than had been used before. All professional recorders and home video cassette recorders made today are based on this technology.

In 1967 Ampex again developed products that created dramatic changes in the video industry. Not only did it introduce the first color portable videotape recorder, it also developed the first color, slow motion, stop-action replay magnetic disc recorder, the Ampex HS-100. This machine's first use was in slow motion and instant replay of sports broadcasts.

Bing Crosby, one of the first backers of Ampex, with an early home tape recorder.

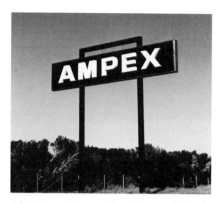

The Ampex sign at the company's head-quarters in Redwood City is a familiar landmark along Highway 101.

Ampex has clearly been a pioneer in the area of video technology. It is unsurpassed in the industry for the number of Emmy awards won for technical achievement in television broadcasting.

Ampex technology is used for a number of purposes other than in the television industry. Ampex products are used in the medical field for diagnosis of certain illnesses and to record and study surgical procedures. They are also found in systems running a stock exchange, a paper mill, and an auto manufacturing foundry. One American railway system uses Ampex digital tape drives as part of a system to locate tracks in need of maintenance.

Other Ampex innovations include the Super High Bit Rate instrumentation recorder, which can record data up to 100 times faster than standard computer tape and disk drives, and a memory device used in the first machine to convert words into synthetic speech for the blind. As a result of these and other developments, Ampex has in excess of 1,900 patents, more than 700 of them in the United States alone.

From its early beginnings as a tiny company with fewer than a dozen employees, Ampex has grown tremendously over the past 40 years. Today the firm has 7,000 employees, and its headquarters cover 55 acres in Redwood City. Ampex has nine sales and service offices in the United States, and 30 throughout the world, selling in 115 countries. It also has a number of manufacturing sites nationwide and abroad in Opelika, Alabama; Colorado Springs, Colorado; and El Segundo, Sunnyvale, and Redwood City, California; as well as in Hong Kong, Taiwan, and Reading, England.

As one of the few very large companies in the area, the Redwood City headquarters of Ampex emphasizes its role as a corporate citizen. Although it is now a large, international corporation, the firm has retained its local ties and supports local organizations and activities that are directly and indirectly beneficial to its employees. It contributes funds and other support to local cultural organizations, various charities, educational institutions, and programs for the disadvantaged, among others.

Ampex Corporation has expanded its focus quite a bit since its early days of airborne radar motors. The company has divided its operations into four divisions: Recording Systems, Video Systems, Magnetic Tape, and Computer Products. These various divisions continue research and development in their areas, as well as blending technologies between divisions to create new innovations in the various industries Ampex serves.

Ampex provides state-of-the-art video equipment to television broadcast stations, networks, and production companies, like the one shown here.

REDWOOD SHORES, INC.

Redwood Shores is one of the few successful new towns that rose from the ashes of the new town movement of the 1960s. The concept of new towns, or planned communities, came about as a method of addressing the problems of increasing urban sprawl. The movement of the middle class out of the inner cities resulted in the creation of new municipalities, all competing for the new tax base of population. Without cooperation and coordinated planning between these cities, urban sprawl was inevitable. To combat this problem, government agencies and large corporations cooperated in obtaining large plots of land and developing entire towns in a controlled manner. The concept was new and exciting, but the reality was too financially burdensome for most corporations to sustain, and most new towns went bankrupt.

Redwood Shores was one of these new towns, established in 1964 by Leslie Properties, Inc., a division of the Leslie Salt Company. The project began with the cooperation and support of Redwood City, but by 1972 this town, too, was bankrupt. Leslie Properties searched for buyers to take over the project, and finally found an interested party in Mobil Land Development Corp. Mobil had studied the project, and many similar ones, and decided to take on the challenge. It sent in a small team to study the area, purchased the property, and, as a result

Redwood Shores Peninsula, adjacent to the Bayshore Freeway. In the forefront is the 3.5-million-square-foot executive office park, Shores Center, with residential development in the background.

of its work, made the project into a successful and vital community.

The success of the project under Mobil can be attributed to two major factors. First, although the firm sent in a small team from its Vancouver office, all additional staff was hired locally. This group did not begin development work immediately. Instead, they became involved in the local community by joining local business and municipal organizations and by studying the unique aspects of the area. Once the team began actual construction in 1978, its members were familiar with and had the support of the local community. The second reason for the success of the project is unique, found in only a few corporations—Mobil could afford to

sustain the financial burden of studying and slowly developing the project without realizing immediate profit. In fact, Redwood Shores became profitable only in 1986. Few corporations could afford this patience, as was evident in the early days of the new town movement.

When Redwood Shores, Inc., finally did begin development, it incorporated many of the ideas of the original new town developers. Neighborhoods were designed around curved streets, rather than in a rectilinear layout. Recreational areas and open space were also incorporated into the design. One of Redwood Shores' first actions was to set aside most of Bair Island, part of the acquired acreage, as a wildlife sanctuary. This area is now the largest blue heron rookery in California. This action set the tone for the rest of the project, which was to "design with nature."

Along these lines, Redwood Shores brought back to life a stagnated and unsafe lagoon dug on the property during the Depression. Redwood Shores installed tide gates, allowing the bay to continuously flush the lagoon. The result was a clean salt-water lake filled with fish and used for recreation by the residents. The company also incorporated more water into the project than originally planned by creating canals

The lagoon with adjacent residential development in the foreground and Shores Center to the rear. Competition is under way in the annual Redwood Shores Standard Rowing Classic, one of the many recreational uses for the lagoon.

for more water frontage and reducing the density of housing.

Redwood Shores' plan included not only the development of homes, but also the inclusion of businesses to provide jobs for the residents. These corporate and service-related businesses were developed adjacent to residential areas to provide an easy commute within Redwood Shores. This aspect of the plan was necessary for addressing a major problem of urban sprawl: bumper-to-

Residents enjoy the lagoon with one of the many beautifully landscaped communities within Redwood Shores in the background.

A typical office building in Shores Center. It was developed by Bolin Development Company of Houston, designed by internationally renowned Tony Lumsden of DMJM, and is the headquarters office of DHL Worldwide Express, an international courier.

bumper commute traffic.

To address the need for affordable housing by lower-income employees, the company worked with Redwood City to create Heron Court, a cooperative housing project. Although the project met initial opposition by local residents, the project gained the support of the city council, and, after Redwood Shores' donation of the land for the housing, the project was completed. Heron Court now has a five-year

waiting list, and has won awards for design and for providing affordable housing in a county where that commodity is increasingly scarce.

Today Redwood Shores is one of the few surviving and successful new towns resulting from the original new town movement. Its continued success comes in part from being owned and developed by one entity rather than by a number of cooperating groups.

Its current size is also easier to manage and creates less environmental impact, reducing the number of tangles with environmental groups. Although Redwood Shores was originally conceived as a home for 100,000 residents, the present plan foresees 20,000 residents. The exclusion of Bair Island from development, fewer children in each family, and the dedication of more land to water rather than to houses all account for the reduction in size.

Redwood Shores also developed stringent controls for builders who contract with it, and has abided by them, resulting in consistently high quality development.

Today Redwood Shores is studied by developers across the country and around the world. It has completed approximately one-third of its final plans, and continues to develop the community according to its original concepts.

Another award-winning town house project illustrates Redwood Shores' talent for creating new waterfront-oriented developments.

BAY VIEW FEDERAL SAVINGS AND LOAN ASSOCIATION

The original office of Bay View Building and Loan Association was in the tiny building on the right in San Francisco's Butchertown.

From a small office in San Francisco's Butchertown to its high-rise headquarters in San Mateo, Bay View Federal Savings and Loan Association has come a long way through challenging times since its founding in 1911. In those post-earthquake days most of downtown San Francisco was rebuilt and back on the road to prosperity. But many residents of outlying, working-class areas had difficulty getting bank loans to rebuild their neighborhoods and buy new homes.

One of those residents was a friend of Fred Zimmerman, who agreed to arrange the loan for him. As a result of this transaction, Zimmerman decided to find a better way for his friends and neighbors to obtain home loans. Later that year he organized a mutual neighborhood association, with each member pledging $700 toward capitalization. This new Bay View Building and Loan Association, as it was called, set up its first offices in a tiny building in the Bay View-Hunters Point district, then known as Butchertown. A local butcher, James Allen, became the association's first president. The organization financed its first home that year—a prefabricated, mail-order cottage.

The motto of the new association was "Our profits are your profits" and, in no time at all, Bay View was able to pay a 7-percent dividend on savings accounts, higher than most associations of this kind in 1915.

But the association was still a relatively small institution, run and staffed by the board of directors. Not until 1917 did Bay View have any full-time employees. Also that year the "Hansen tradition" of Bay View leadership began when Carl and Samuel Hansen joined the board of directors. The Hansen fam-ily continued to head the company through much of its history.

By 1919 Bay View Building & Loan Association had grown to the point that it had to move to new headquarters across the street. There it continued to prosper until hit by the effects of the stock market crash of 1929. The association did not actually feel the effects until 1930, the same year that Carl Hansen's son, Leslie, became secretary of Bay View. By this time borrowers were having great difficulty making their monthly payments, and Leslie devised a plan that allowed the borrowers to pay back any amount possible, rather than lose their homes. The association also had to lower its dividend rate, and made no new loans for three years.

In 1935 Leslie Hansen led the association's conversion to a federal association, which would allow it to receive funds invested by the U.S. Treasury. The name was changed to

The grand opening of Bay View Federal Savings' South San Francisco branch, the first branch in San Mateo County.

Bay View Federal Savings and Loan Association. Soon a third generation of Hansens joined the bank when Leslie's son, Elwood, took a job as a teller.

Bay View continued to grow profitably until World War II, when it was hard hit by strict governmental controls on nonessential building. With the number of loans reduced, the association once again had to lower the dividend rate and had to restrict savings deposits. But through repaid loans and War Bond sales, Leslie Hansen was able to lead Bay View successfully through the war years.

Leslie Hansen died the day before D day, having taken the association through almost 20 years of very challenging economic times that saw the assets of the bank increase by more than $3 million. His son, Elwood, had a tough act to follow when he took his father's post two weeks later. But the economic climate was favorable, and postwar prosperity created a huge home-building boom. Bay View was able to underwrite millions of dollars worth of home loans.

The year 1954 was the beginning of a new chapter in the history of Bay View. Elwood Hansen became president, and Bay View's aggressive expansion program began with the opening of its first branch office in San Francisco's Richmond District.

Expansion continued rapidly for the next 20 years. Bay View soon opened its first San Mateo County offices in South San Francisco and Millbrae. By 1978 Bay View had opened 24 branches both north and south of San Francisco, and had moved its headquarters to the present site in the city of San Mateo. Three years later Bay View had 41 branches throughout the San Francisco Bay Area. The fourth generation of Hansens had also arrived on the scene: In 1980 Robert Hansen became president of Bay View.

The 1980s began yet another period of great change and challenge for Bay View. Deregulation and inflation forced the restructuring of the entire financial community, and Bay

View was no exception. Competition became intense among banks, savings and loans, and brokerages, where before there had been little. Many financial institutions were forced to close. Bay View's solution was to reorganize and consolidate its offices. Many branches were sold, closed, or combined. The first non-Hansen was hired to lead Bay View: Robert Barnes became the organization's new president. The bank also converted from a mutual association to a stock association in 1986.

Today Bay View has completed its restructuring process and has 18 profitable branches, five of them in San Mateo County. It is no longer

The headquarters of Bay View Federal Savings is located in San Mateo in the Bay View Plaza.

just a provider of home loans and savings accounts, but a service-oriented savings and loan that offers everything from consumer loans, savings, and checking accounts to IRAs, money market accounts, and alternative investments. Its main stronghold is now on the San Mateo County peninsula. With more than 300 employees today, Bay View Federal Savings and Loan Association is ready for whatever changes and challenges the future holds.

GENENTECH, INC.

Genentech is not a very old company, but its place in history is already assured. The firm was the first to develop products using recombinant DNA technology for commercial purposes. Recombinant DNA technology is an aspect of genetic engineering based on recombining genes from different organisms to make new forms of DNA.

Genentech uses this technology to develop treatments for diseases that were formerly untreatable or treatments that were only available in limited supply. The company's scientists are able to make proteins in larger quantities than are normally made in the human body to use in fighting diseases and disorders.

Recombinant DNA technology was originally developed in 1973 by Herbert Boyer and Stanley Cohen, professors with the University of California and Stanford University, respectively, as a method that could

Analysis of laboratory assays by a Genentech scientist helps to determine the effectiveness of a new pharmaceutical produced through recombinant DNA technology.

aid researchers in the study of heredity. They patented this method as the Cohen Boyer method.

Robert Swanson had more extensive plans for this technology. A venture capitalist with Kleiner Perkins, he was convinced that the Cohen Boyer method would be commercially viable for pharmaceuticals. In a short but fateful meeting in a San Francisco bar, Swanson convinced Boyer that this idea was feasible, and the two of them pledged $500 each toward the founding of their new pharmaceuticals venture. With an initial investment by Kleiner Perkins as well, they opened Genentech in 1976 in a rented San Francisco office with one employee.

After only a year the company had its first breakthrough. Using recombinant DNA technology Genentech scientists were the first to clone and express (express means to produce a protein) somatostatin, a brain protein normally made by the human body. This protein was not developed as a commercial product, but rather to prove that useful proteins could be made using this technology.

In 1978 the organization successfully cloned human insulin, marking another first. This product is extremely valuable for the treatment of diabetes. Before Genentech researchers cloned and expressed the human hormone, it was obtained from the pancreas of pigs and cows; unfortunately, many diabetics are al-

Genentech, located in South San Francisco, is the largest multi-product recombinant DNA pharmaceuticals plant in the world.

lergic to this form of insulin. Human insulin is, of course, perfectly natural to the human body, and ultimately was the first product of recombinant DNA technology to be approved by the Food and Drug Administration in 1982. At the time Genentech was too small to market its products, so it licensed the insulin to the Eli Lilly pharmaceutical company. Today nearly half of all newly diagnosed diabetics receive human insulin.

Genentech moved to San Mateo County in 1978 and set up shop in a South San Francisco warehouse. This location was chosen because of the low cost, and because it was centrally located among the major universities and near the airport. A year later the firm became the first profitable biotechnology operation.

In 1980, after only a year of profitability and with no product yet on the market, Genentech made investment history as well. The corporation was the first biotechnology firm to go public. It opened at $35 a share and in only 20 minutes rocketed to $88 per share, an unbroken record on Wall Street.

Another milestone came in 1985, when the FDA approved the company's human growth hormone—Protropin. It can be used to combat short stature in children with growth hormone deficiency, a result of the pituitary gland's inability to produce enough growth hormone. At one time the hormone was extracted from pituitary glands of cadavers, but had been removed from the market when it was linked to fatalities. When Protropin was approved no other human growth hormone was available to treat the children who needed it.

Protropin was the first product that Genentech was able to clone, express, manufacture, and market. The firm's full-scale manufacturing facilities had been in operation since 1983, and growing rapidly. The company was now large enough to handle all aspects of product development from start to finish.

Genentech's most recent product—approved for the market in 1987—is Activase, a protein that dissolves blood clots. Approved as a treatment for heart attacks, the protein begins to work immediately upon injection and can stop a heart attack in progress.

In anticipation of Activase's approval, the company completed construction in 1986 of a huge manufacturing facility the size of two

football fields dedicated to the manufacture of Activase. Genentech now has the largest multi-product recombinant DNA pharmaceuticals plant in the world.

The corporation is continually re-

Vials of freeze-dried product manufactured through recombinant DNA technology.

Genentech's 100,000-square-foot manufacturing facility provides the company with uniquely versatile capabilities in process development, fermentation, recovery, and purification of products manufactured by genetically engineered microbes. Shown here are process development and fermentation staff members, who are monitoring conditions for the manufacturing of many proteins now in preclinical and human testing.

searching new pharmaceuticals in three major areas: molecular immunology, cardiovascular biology, and developmental biology. Currently Genentech scientists are conducting studies with two products, gamma interferon and tumor necrosis factor, to determine their effectiveness in fighting cancer. The organization also has an active program for the treatment and prevention of AIDS. Included in its research programs are cooperative agreements with universities and training programs for university faculty and postdoctoral students. The company sells its products domestically through direct sales to major medical centers and hospitals. Abroad, Genentech has agreements with a number of pharmaceutical firms to distribute its products worldwide.

CUNHA'S COUNTRY STORE

Cunha's Country Store serves as a community information center, as a meeting place for old friends, and reflects a sense of local history as well. Beverly Marie Cunha Ashcraft has run the store that way for more than 27 years, as her father, William P. Cunha, did before her.

The Cunha name is well known in Half Moon Bay. William Cunha, a third-generation Half Moon Bay resident, purchased the general store business from his employer in 1929, with $1,000 from a cashed-in insurance policy. His brother ran a feed, fuel, and insurance business next door, and another brother-in-law owned a livery stable and drove a stagecoach between San Mateo and Half Moon Bay. The local school still carries the Cunha name.

Cunha's store occupied the first floor of the building that it is still in today. The second floor was a dance hall where the volunteer fire department held its dances until the late 1930s.

The store served a community made up mostly of farmers, providing groceries and dry goods, as well as farming tools and other supplies. Half Moon Bay was an insular town; supplies came to the store by freight

Beverly Marie Cunha Ashcraft, the founder's daughter, currently owns and operates Cunha's Country Store.

wagon over what is now Highway 92, and by sea at nearby Miramar pier.

Today Cunha's is still a general store serving the needs of the community. The supplies still come to the store over Highway 92, although now they arrive in trucks run by the Fleming Company. The store still provides groceries and dry goods, changed to meet the needs of a town no longer based on farming. Cunha's sells goods to a very diverse population, including people of Japanese, Chinese, Portuguese, and Spanish descent, as well as a large number of visiting tourists. Cunha's purchases supplies from a number of specialty companies around the peninsula to supplement its stock.

Twelve years ago Beverly Ashcraft bought the building, one of the oldest in Half Moon Bay, and remodeled the facilities to modernize them and bring them up to code. The cathedral ceiling upstairs has been lowered, and the dance hall stage holds western wear instead of dancing feet. Modern refrigerators and shelving cover the old hardwood floors, which have creaked under generations of customers. Local customers can still pay their bills monthly, as the farmers did when William Cunha ran the store.

The basic purpose of the store has remained the same, however. It has always been a general store and community center. Beverly provides

Cunha's is still the general store and community center of Half Moon Bay.

William P. Cunha, founder.

not only merchandise, but information and personal service as well. She knows most people in town, and is a reservoir of information. Need a babysitter? Ask Beverly for a recommendation. Looking for an apartment? Someone at Cunha's may know of one. Trying to find a special wine? Cunha's can order it for you. Beverly is at the store daily and keeps it open seven days a week from 8 a.m. to 8 p.m.

Before the Alpha Beta and Safeway grocery stores established business in town, Cunha's was one of a very few small local grocery stores. Today the large supermarkets represent undeniable competition for Cunha's Country Store. But one thing they can not provide is the personalized touch, the knowledge of the community, and the individual service. Go to Cunha's for that.

COTCHETT & ILLSTON

Now in its third decade on the San Mateo peninsula, the law offices of Cotchett & Illston have been active in all segments of the San Mateo County community. Founded in San Mateo by Joseph Cotchett—a Hastings graduate and former paratrooper captain—the firm has grown to nearly 40 people, and moved to its own building in Burlingame, next to the San Francisco Airport. With an additional office in Los Angeles, being near the airport is important to the firm; it has both a statewide and a national trial practice, with many clients in Southern California. "On any given Monday morning some of our people are at the airport, flying to Los Angeles, San Diego, or New York," says Susan Illston, a Phi Beta Kappa and Stanford law graduate, as well as the managing partner of the firm.

The firm today specializes in civil litigation. Its cases include consumer and investment frauds, securities, antitrust, construction, property

From left: Frank Pitre, Susan Illston, Alan Haverty, and Joseph Cotchett. The three senior partners are shown here with Alan Haverty, the newest lawyer to join the firm. Haverty was a San Mateo County judge for more than 14 years.

and personal damage cases, and matters that relate to litigation in the courts. While initially concerned solely with peninsula clients, Cotchett & Illston's clientele now reads like a who's who in California.

The firm is generally hired as special trial counsel on specific cases, and has represented some of the largest corporations in the country. Such companies include GAF Corporation, Paramount Studios, and Union Bank in Los Angeles, to name a few. It has also represented public agencies as special trial counsel, such as the State of South Dakota in antitrust matters. Other clients have included the National Football League and various NFL teams. A number of notable individuals have sought representation from the firm, including sports celebrities, entertainers, and various elected officials such as members of the state assembly and the senate.

Cotchett & Illston also represents many members of the public, often on a no-fee basis, who simply need representation in worthwhile cases. "Many of the cases we handle have great social value, since they usually involve matters that affect a broad cross section of the community," says Frank Pitre, a young partner in the firm.

Cotchett & Illston is located at the San Francisco Airport Office Center Building adjacent to the San Francisco International Airport.

Members of the firm have been extremely active in professional and community associations on the peninsula. This includes the San Mateo Boys and Girls Club, the Heart Association, hospital advisory boards, the Legal Aid Society, the YMCA, the Service League of San Mateo County, the State Bar Board of Governors, the Judicial Council of the State of California, and various commissions and agencies. Lawyers in the firm have also handled matters for a number of charitable organizations and worthwhile causes. A recent addition to the firm is retired judge Alan Haverty, who served on the San Mateo County bench for more than 14 years before joining Cotchett & Illston.

The firm has been involved in some of the largest investment fraud cases on the West Coast, and has handled some very celebrated cases. All of the lawyers are actively involved in professional organizations as authors and speakers. Some of the books and articles written by firm members are considered to be leading authorities in the profession on trial law and related subjects. Cotchett & Illston excels because of its people, as outstanding lawyers, and more important, as active members of the community.

THE PENINSULA REGENT

When healthy, active, senior citizens are tired of maintaining their San Mateo homes, yet do not want to leave their community, what options do they have for retirement living? The developers of BAC Associates hope to provide one answer with The Peninsula Regent, a senior housing community scheduled to open October 1988 in San Mateo.

The Peninsula Regent was developed by BAC Associates, a limited partnership whose general partners' corporate executives come from three of the most respected development firms in the Bay Area: Gerson Bakar & Associates, Pacific Union Development Company, and Liberty Management Company, Inc.

BAC conducted extensive research nationwide to determine what motivated people to move into retirement communities, and what features they looked for in those communities. After extensive study, BAC chose the city of San Mateo as the ideal site for development, be-

cause it has a large, established older population and plenty of shopping, services, and other amenities in the area. Once San Mateo was chosen, BAC also consulted with experts in gerontology and with local residents to complete the research process.

The design phase of The Peninsula Regent was undertaken by Backen, Arrigoni & Ross, a San Francisco-based architectural firm. The company designed the building in a cruciform to set residences back from the street, enhance the view from the residences, and provide for large, separate outdoor landscapes. The developers broke ground in October 1986, and have remained on schedule in their construction plans.

In this location BAC hopes to develop a flagship life care community that will be responsive to the needs of its residents. BAC, along with BRIDGE Housing Corporation, a nonprofit developer experienced in hous-

ing construction, designed The Peninsula Regent around a resident membership program. It appointed Bay Area Senior Services (BASS), a nonprofit group created by BRIDGE, to lease the facilities and manage The Peninsula Regent as a membership program in cooperation with an advisory board of residents.

At present the advisory board consists of BASS-appointed community leaders. The board holds "focus group" meetings with the future Regent member residents as new issues arise for discussion. Based on the decisions made in these meetings, BASS will provide a number of features and has implemented a number of changes to the program requested by the future residents. With complete occupancy of the

---

Charter members at the groundbreaking ceremony for The Peninsula Regent in October 1986.

community, the present advisory board will be replaced by the resident advisory board. Future members currently receive a periodic newsletter to keep them informed of the Regent's progress. The members also attend social events to familiarize themselves with their future neighbors.

One common concern that BAC discovered in its research, and has addressed, is that seniors want to retain equity even after moving into the Regent, or any other senior community. Many traditional life care systems require a large, nonrefundable initial deposit. Residents who sell their homes and move into these programs lose their equity if they choose to leave. At the Regent, residents pay a one-time fee to a membership that can later be sold. Monthly service fees cover the actual cost of operating The Peninsula

Regent.

Another of the programs designed especially for The Peninsula Regent residents is the health care program. This program stresses wellness and preventive medicine. All applicants to the resident program undergo initial health screenings. Home health care is promoted, and members are encouraged to retain their own physicians. The Regent will provide a group insurance policy with broad coverage, which would be unavailable to members as individuals. The Regent will also have an on-site medical director who can design individual wellness plans for the members, as well as on-site, short-term health care facilities. BASS has arranged an agreement with nearby Mills-Peninsula Hospital to provide longer term and acute care for residents if necessary.

The Regent plans to provide a

The Peninsula Regent provides an ideal solution for retirement living.

number of recreational activities, again based on the desires of the residents. The grounds will include an outdoor croquet lawn, a greenhouse for gardening, a restaurant with outdoor seating, and an enclosed swimming pool and spa. The Peninsula Regent also plans to provide a residents' services coordinator on site. The coordinator's function will be to arrange activities the residents propose. Specially arranged transportation to these activities, as well as regularly scheduled service, will be available to residents.

For many San Mateo residents, The Peninsula Regent will soon provide an ideal solution for retirement living.

THE TIMES (THE SAN MATEO TIMES)

The Times (The San Mateo Times), which will celebrate its centennial in 1989, is the only daily newspaper published in San Mateo County today. But that was not always the case. The paper has gone through many mergers and transformations before becoming *The Times* read today.

The paper has its origins in the *San Mateo Leader,* a weekly founded in April 1889. The first issue of the *San Mateo Leader* contained a "salutatory," as the editors called it, which expressed the intent of the new publication: . . . the interests of San Mateo and vicinity and of the northern and coast sections of the county are sufficiently important to deserve representation in the newspaper field . . . The *Leader* will be . . . energetic and progressive in advancing the interests of the county and advertising to the world the resources and attractions of this section, and ever alive to the comprehensive publication of local news and all that is readable to our residents.

The paper was founded by Charles Kirkbride, age 20, and Charles Jury, age 17, former employees of the *San Jose Mercury.* Despite their youth and relative lack of experience, the newspaper did quite well. Kirkbride stayed in the business for a year, after which he sold his interest in the paper to Jury. Jury ran the paper until 1909, when he finally sold the business to H.W. Simpkins, the editor of the *Palo Alto Times.*

After three more ownership transfers, the *San Mateo Leader* ended up in the hands of J.D. Bromfield, a later editor of the *Palo Alto Times,* and A.P. Bellisle, the *Leader's* business manager. While continuing to publish the *Leader* as a weekly paper, Bromfield and Bellisle launched the first daily paper in the county, the *Daily San Mateo County News.* In 1917 Bromfield bought Bellisle's interest in the company, and soon combined the two papers into the *Daily News Leader.*

During the course of all these buyouts and management changes, Robert Thompson had started a sec-

Horace A. Amphlett, founder of Amphlett Printing Company, which publishes the **San Mateo Times** *(top left).*

J. Hart Clinton, publisher of the **San Mateo Times** *for 40 years (top right).*

John Clinton is the current publisher of the **San Mateo Times** *(left).*

ond weekly paper, the *San Mateo Times,* in 1901. It, too, went through a series of ownership transfers until it was acquired by Horace A. Amphlett. Amphlett, although he was an accomplished poet and playwright, was not an experienced newspaperman. He had been a postmaster and then an employee of the San Mateo National Bank. Nevertheless, he ran the paper so successfully that in 1924 it began printing daily.

By this time four daily papers were in circulation in the county—the *San Mateo Times,* the *Daily News Leader,* and two Burlingame papers: *The Advance* and *The Star.* This was a bad situation for all four papers and for local merchants

as well. Competition was tough, and local readers were so divided among the papers that merchants were forced to advertise in more than one publication. A group of local businessmen formed a merchants committee and requested that the papers merge to alleviate the problem. As a result, Amphlett purchased the *Daily News Leader* in 1926 and combined it with *The Times,* making the full name of the paper the *San Mateo Times and Daily News Leader.* The Burlingame papers combined as well and became *The Advance-Star.*

Regardless of all these mergers and takeovers, the purpose and focus of the *San Mateo Times and Daily News Leader* remained relatively constant since its first days as the *San Mateo Leader.* Amphlett stated his views on running the paper when he said: "Only such newspapers as fill a definite need in the community, supporting its institutions, safeguarding its interests, and protecting its character abroad, can hope to endure."

In 1930 Amphlett incorporated the Amphlett Printing Company and transferred his interest in the paper to the corporation. Amphlett died a few years later, and for 10 years the paper was published by the trust he had established in his will. This period was the height of the Great Depression, and the paper had tough competition from *The Advance-Star* and from another daily paper, the *Redwood City Tribune.* As a result, the *San Mateo Times and Daily News Leader* produced no dividends until 1936.

In 1944 J. Hart Clinton, Amphlett's brother-in-law, became publisher of the paper, a position he was to hold for 40 years. Clinton led the paper through years in which its competition decreased and its circulation increased.

In 1964 the paper built its present facilities, including a publishing plant, on what is now Amphlett Boulevard. The typesetting process was also modernized dramatically.

For 30 years **The Times** *operated out of this building on Second Street in San Mateo before moving to its present offices in 1964.*

With the old system, which used "hot metal," seven or eight lines of type could be set each minute. When the system was modernized, it produced 400 to 600 lines of type per minute. This change resulted in the need for fewer employees to produce the paper.

In 1973 the Amphlett Printing Company purchased the name and

A peninsula landmark, **The Times'** *present building in San Mateo is off the Bayshore Freeway.*

goodwill of *The Advance-Star,* which had ceased publication, and incorporated the name into the masthead of *The Times.* The full name on the masthead today, in addition to *The Times,* is *San Mateo Times* and *Daily News Leader/The Advance Star.*

By the time John Clinton, J. Hart's son, became publisher in 1987, *The Times* had grown dramatically from assets of $197,000 to $8.3 million. Its paid circulation in 1944 was 4,000; today it is approximately 45,000. The paper publishes four editions for its readers—the street edition, the North County edition, the South County edition, and the Central County edition. Not only is it the only daily newspaper published in the county, it is the only independent, locally owned daily paper in the San Francisco Bay Area.

John Clinton estimates that one-third of the paper's readers depend only on *The Times* for all their newspaper news. The paper continues to remain true to its original purpose, emphasizing local news, but also providing a broad selection of state, national, and international news for its readers.

SUNSET MAGAZINE

Sunset Magazine has covered the western United States since its founding by the Southern Pacific Railroad in 1898. Named for the Sunset Limited train between New Orleans and Los Angeles, the magazine was originated by the railroad to promote tourism, agriculture, and industry in the western region. *Sunset* circulated nationally, urging its readers to invest in the West. Southern Pacific was one of the largest landholders and speculators in the region, and early articles in its magazine discussed the attractions of California, Oregon, Nevada, Texas, Louisiana, and the territories of Arizona and New Mexico, through which Southern Pacific's train lines ran.

These promotional articles described various western communities and the ideal qualities of each. The scenic beauty of Santa Cruz, the agricultural bounty of Napa Valley, and the mineral wealth of Baker City were all presented in tempting detail in *Sunset's* pages. Of course, most of the advertisements and articles mentioned the convenience of the railroad lines connecting these communities.

San Mateo County was included in *Sunset's* pages from the publica-

Lane Publishing Co., which produces **Sunset Magazine,** **Sunset Books,** *and* **Sunset Films & Television,** *is presently owned by L. W. "Bill" Lane, Jr. (left), on leave as U.S. Ambassador to Australia; Melvin B. Lane (right), chairman of Lane Publishing Co.; and their families. Behind them is a portrait of their parents, Laurence W. Lane, Sr., and Ruth Bell Lane, founders of Lane Publishing Co. The portrait was presented to them on the 38th anniversary of the company's founding.*

tion's earliest days. A series of 1907 articles by Rufus Steele, entitled "The Spread of San Francisco," discussed the benefits of living in San Mateo County—an area once reserved for the estates of the very wealthy. With the advent of faster, more convenient Southern Pacific train lines through the county, Steele stressed that the workingman could enjoy country living and still commute easily into San Francisco each day. He wrote: "Go visit these places for yourself and when you have reveled in the natural beauty of down the peninsula, when you have felt your heart stirring at the thought of what home life might be in such homes, when you have loitered through lanes and paths and

avenues that have no equal anywhere—then doubtless, you shall understand how the march of progress which brings these communities . . . within reach of the workers of a great city is more than a commercial consideration."

In 1914 Southern Pacific sold the magazine to its employees. Although *Sunset* had always carried literary pieces in addition to its promotional articles, the new owners changed the magazine's emphasis to a literary one by soliciting the works of well-known and soon-to-be well-known writers from all over the West. This focus promoted the West in a new way by exhibiting the cultural wealth of the region. Contributors to the magazine included Jack London, Bret Harte, Sinclair Lewis, and John Muir.

Without the backing of the railroad, *Sunset* was never able to retain the financial success it had enjoyed under the ownership of Southern Pacific. It survived for 14 years, but by that time was having financial problems too great to resolve on its own.

The first issue of **Sunset Magazine,** *published by the Southern Pacific Company in 1898. The magazine at that time was a promotional tool to encourage travel and migration to the West. The cover is a view of the San Francisco Bay featuring the Golden Gateway before the bridge was built.*

The publication was revived under the guidance of Laurence W. Lane, who bought it for $65,000 in 1928. During the first 10 years of Lane's guidance, the magazine's format and direction changed dramatically. *Sunset* was divided into four major categories—building, gardening, travel, and cooking—which still define the periodical today. Lane regionalized it into three editions tailored to readers' life-styles in the Northwest, Central, and Southern California regions (Hawaii was later added to the Southern California region), and although the magazine had always served the desert resident, a separate desert edition was introduced in 1963. *Sunset* became an informational, "how-to" magazine written completely by the staff for westerners alone.

Lane also published the first of the hundreds of *Sunset* books, the *Kitchen Cabinet Book* in 1932. Where once it had served to promote the West to the rest of the world, now *Sunset Magazine* was written for westerners to bring them the latest information on western living. At the end of those 10 years the magazine was in the black for the first time since being run by South-

The front entrance to the South Building of the Lane Publishing Co. headquarters at the corner of Willow and Middlefield roads in Menlo Park. The pine doors were hand carved on the premises in 1951 as the building was being completed.

ern Pacific. The publication introduced its readers to new styles in architecture, to new regional foods, to new gardening techniques, and to new vacation spots.

In the 1950s San Mateo County appeared in its pages in an article on picnic places. By this time there was no longer any need to promote the county as an ideal homesite. It was already experiencing its tremendous postwar building boom. Now the emphasis was on how to escape the crowds.

In 1951 *Sunset* moved its offices from San Francisco to Menlo Park. The magazine's audience was mostly a suburban one, and the Lanes believed the editors could identify with their readers more closely from a suburban environment than from an urban one. The setting also allowed the magazine to expand and to develop its "laboratory of western living," with test kitchens and experimental gardens. Eventually the expansive, landscaped grounds became a favorite spot for sightseers, and *Sunset* has provided guided tours for more than 20 years.

During the 1950s *Sunset* also began taking a more active role in conservation. Whereas the magazine had always stressed the appreciation of natural beauty, it was now beginning to address conservation issues

directly. San Mateo County has figured in this concern. Over the years articles featuring scenic spots along the San Mateo coastline have alerted readers to issues affecting its environment: oil drilling, uncontrolled development, and land-planning decisions by the state legislature. *Sunset Magazine* was also a major supporter of the creation of Butano State Park in San Mateo County, one of the few stands of virgin redwood in the state.

Today—under the name of Lane Publishing Co., headed by Laurence's sons, L.W. "Bill" and Melvin B. Lane—*Sunset Magazine* is distributed in 13 western states to more than 5 million readers. The Sunset Book division has more than 200 titles in print that are sold nationally and internationally, and a newer division, Sunset Films & Television, has produced more than 125 films. The magazine of the West has become the magazine for the West, and it continues to bring to its readers the last word on western living.

The first issue of **Sunset Magazine** *under Lane family ownership, February 1929. The cover was painted by Maurice Logan and is a view of Lake Tahoe.*

GELSAR

Carl (left) and Fred Gellert, founders of the Standard Building Company, discuss construction plans for their Sunstream homes.

In 1968, when shoppers started coming to Serramonte Center, it was unique in being one of the first completely enclosed climate-controlled shopping centers in the country. Today, with 152 tenants, it is one of the larger and most successful shopping centers in San Mateo County. It is owned and managed by Gelsar, a real estate management company with roots in a home-building business started by Fred and Carl Gellert in 1922.

Fred Gellert and his older brother Carl were both born in San Francisco. Children of poor immigrant parents, they had to start their working careers at an early age. The only time they had for a regular school education was at night. At age 14 Fred was working as a welder in the Union Iron Works shipyard and delivering newspapers on the weekends. Later he and Carl worked with their father painting houses. From this house-painting experience they were inspired to go into the home-building business together.

In 1922, after saving their earnings for many years, the brothers decided to buy a lot on 28th Avenue near Judah Street in San Francisco and subcontract with tradesmen to build a house on it. This venture turned out successfully when they sold the house at a profit. The Standard Building Company was established and continued as a small business, buying lots and building homes on them throughout the 1920s and into the Great Depression, when house buying and building slowed drastically. With a lot of ef-fort and much personal sacrifice on the part of the Gellert brothers, the firm survived the Depression.

The onset of World War II did not help the home-building industry either—the government controlled building materials at that time, and almost no private construction occurred. Standard Building was able to stay in business by obtaining government contracts to build military barracks and other housing units on Treasure Island, in Pittsburg, and in Stockton for military personnel and government employees.

It was after World War II when the Gellert brothers' business experienced its greatest growth. The return of military personnel to the Bay Area plus a pent-up demand for new homes led to a tremendous home-building boom, which helped Standard Building Company's rapid growth. Another factor was the philosophy of the firm to construct well-designed, quality homes, affordable to most people. Standard sold these houses under the trademarked name of Sunstream Homes, a product name well known, respected, and sought after in San Francisco and San Mateo counties.

The Gellerts' first San Mateo County homes were built after the war in San Bruno. Later on they had housing developments in Daly City, Millbrae, and South San Francisco.

Fred Gellert, one of the founders of the Standard Building Company, whose family now owns and manages Gelsar, an offshoot of Standard.

It was during the 1950s, when the company was building as many as 500 homes per year, that it started the practice of creating small, independent firms for each construction project. Management and supervisory employees were given the opportunity to buy stock at favorable prices when these new firms were created. During this period of rapid construction, there were as many as 44 companies involved with Standard projects, providing various services such as land development, building construction, real estate, and other support services.

Also during the 1950s Standard began diversifying its activities. Instead of building only single-family homes, the firm entered into the business of building, owning, and managing apartment buildings. Apartment construction helped the company hedge itself against the lows of the home-building cycles and, at the same time, provided much-needed housing for those who could not afford to purchase a new home. Standard developed two small shopping areas in San Francisco that preceded the development of Serramonte—one on Vicente Street and Lakeshore Plaza on Sloat Boulevard. Three office buildings on 19th Avenue in San Francisco were also built, owned, and managed by the company.

In 1958 the Gellerts formed two philanthropic foundations, The Fred Gellert Foundation and The Carl Gellert Foundation, for the purpose of giving financial help to the commu-

nities in which they had prospered. These foundations still donate funds to local cities, charities, and non-profit organizations.

In the early 1960s Standard Building Company decided to enter into a joint venture with the Crocker Land Company for the purpose of acquiring the large Christian Dairy Ranch in Daly City and develop it into an entirely new community of houses, apartments, parks, schools, and shopping centers. Suburban Realty Company was the name of the joint venture, and Serramonte was the name created for the new community. Standard's companies built the houses and apartments, while Crocker handled the development of Serramonte Center, King Center, and part of the commercial area on Gellert Boulevard near Serramonte Boulevard.

These Sunstream homes in Daly City are just some of the thousands of homes Standard Building Company has constructed in Northern California.

Serramonte Center, one of the first completely enclosed, climate-controlled shopping centers in the country. Photo by Scott Bushman

Serramonte Center first opened for business in 1968 with approximately 110 tenants, including Macy's, Montgomery Ward, QFI Market, and Longs Drugs. In 1971 Suburban obtained complete ownership of the center by buying out Foremost McKesson's interest. (Foremost had acquired Crocker's interest at an earlier date.) In 1972 Suburban constructed an addition to the center, which now houses Mervyn's and additional retail stores.

The firm began consolidating its operation in the 1970s by reducing the number of subsidiary firms by nearly half. In the late 1970s Standard started building homes in a large development located in the city of Hercules. Fred Gellert died in 1978, four years after his brother Carl's death. Shortly afterward, in 1980, Standard split its operations. An employee group retained the home-building business and kept its offices in San Francisco. The Fred Gellert family—Fred's widow, Gisela; his son, Fred Gellert, Jr.; and his daughter, Joan Sargen—retained management of the commercial interests under the name of Gelsar and moved its offices to the present location near Serramonte Center.

At the time of the split Standard Building Company and other Gellert firms had built approximately 20,000 Sunstream homes, 1,400 apartment units, 3 shopping centers, and office buildings in various San Mateo and San Francisco locations.

BAY CITY FLOWER COMPANY

Emigrating from Japan to America to make his fortune in 1907, Nobuo Higaki probably had no idea the road to success would be carpeted with flowers. The young man became the founder of Higaki Nursery/ Bay City Flower Company, now a successful potted plant nursery in Half Moon Bay.

At the age of 19 Higaki left his home in Kochi prefecture, a rural community that offered him few economic opportunities. He arrived in Seattle and took a job as a houseboy, then tried his hand at the lumbering business near Spokane. Soon after, he heard from a former classmate, then living in San Francisco, who suggested Higaki join him in starting a flower-growing business. Neither of them knew much about flowers, so their first step was to serve apprenticeships with the McClellan orchid company.

Apparently, the apprenticeships were worthwhile—in 1910 the two men opened a nursery in Redwood City, an area known for its ideal climate. Although the partnership split up shortly afterward, Higaki continued the business as the Higaki Nursery.

In those days the nursery grew carnations, roses, chrysanthemums, and gardenias for florists in San Francisco. To get the flowers to market, Higaki packed the cut flowers in straw baskets, and took them by train to his customers.

The business flourished until it felt the effects of the Depression. Flowers were a luxury item, and times were lean for the nursery. The business suffered yet another setback when the United States entered World War II in 1941. When Japanese-Americans were evacuated from the West Coast, Higaki was interned in a relocation camp, and his wife and six children moved to Idaho to stay with friends. Three of the boys were drafted, and the rest of the family grew produce on Idaho farmland. The Higakis were able to lease the nursery to the Zappettini family until they could return to Redwood City at the war's end.

After the war the nursery grew only cut gardenias for a short time before incorporating as Bay City Flowers, and then converting to potted plants in 1951. Around this time

Higaki retired from the business, and his son Harry became president. Together with brothers Juiichi, Shigeru, and Naomi, they forged ahead as the second generation of the Higaki flower growers.

In the 1950s San Mateo County was experiencing its postwar building boom, and the increasing urbanization of the area was detrimental to the nursery's operation. Housing took priority over business growth, and the nursery found it difficult to expand. It had expanded by opening a branch in Sunnyvale, but that was not sufficient for the company's needs. The increased population in the area was also accompanied by increasing vandalism of the nursery's property, and the Higakis finally decided it was time to move. After consulting with the San Mateo County farm adviser, Hank Sciaroni, Higaki Nursery moved across the county to Half Moon Bay.

Nobuo Higaki (right) and Mr. and Mrs. Kotoharu Inouye (seated with baby and second from left, respectively) and the first delivery truck in 1916.

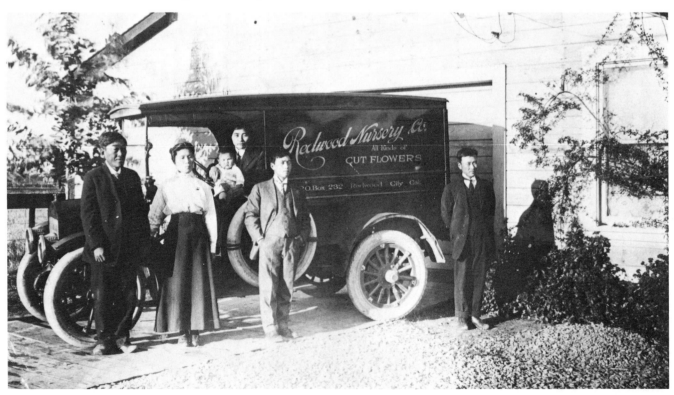

Nobuo Higaki (right) and Kotaharu Inouye (second from left) check the carnation crop in the first greenhouse. Photo circa 1913

Although Half Moon Bay was isolated at the time, and the family was concerned about the lack of transportation and modern utilities, the move turned out to be ideal for the firm's success. The moderate and consistent climate is ideal for growing potted plants, and the availability of land would allow the company to expand its operations—and expand it did.

The climate allowed Bay City Flower to grow many different crops year-round that its competitors in other parts of the state and the nation are unable to grow. On its 100-acre grounds the nursery grows freesias, carnations, cyclamen, tulips, lilies, roses, hydrangeas, poinsettias, and miniature Christmas trees. Bay City Flowers is especially proud of its potted freesias.

Partly due to the favorable climate, the nursery was able to perfect the cultivation of dwarfed potted freesias in the mid-1980s. Before this time these plants were usually sold as cut flowers, because it is very difficult to grow potted freesias to a desirably small size. Bay City

Flower's freesias are also some of the few potted plants that have a fragrance.

When Bay City Flowers moved to Half Moon Bay, it changed its marketing strategy as well. Instead of selling to local florists, the nursery began selling wholesale to supermarket chains. The company supplies its flowers under the trademarked name Hana Bay Flowers (Hana is the Japanese word for flower) to major supermarkets around the country. Its customers include Lucky's, Safeway, Albertson's, Alpha Beta, Raley's, and many others.

Harrison Higaki, Harry's son, became the third generation of the family to lead Bay City Flowers. He began by helping his father when he finished college in 1974, and liked the business so much he returned to school to study horticulture/business administration. Today Harrison is president of Bay City Flower Company. Naomi's son, Ron, who earned a B.A. in business administration, also runs the company's daily operations. Harry acts as chairman

of the board.

From the founder's modest start almost 80 years ago, the Higaki family and loyal associates nurtured Bay City Flowers into a successful business with seemingly few limits to its continued growth. One challenge Harry Higaki anticipates for the future will be finding new ways to work within the government's environmental controls on pesticides and other government restrictions.

The nursery, whose slogan is Bringing Beauty to Life, continues to grow its potted plants and expand its operations. No longer required to deliver its products by train, the firm distributes by truck on a national scale.

The Higakis and their associates feel fortunate to be able to enrich people's lives with some of God's beautiful creations—plants and flowers—and they hope to do so for a long time to come.

UNITED AIRLINES

The growth of the San Francisco International Airport is inextricably linked to the history of United Airlines, the oldest airline in the country. Both were first starting up in the fledgling commercial airline business only 20 years after the Wright brothers flew the first mechanically powered airborne vehicle. Today the San Francisco International Airport in San Mateo County is one of the most important links for United routes. Not only is it one of the busiest airports for United and an important gateway for flights to the Pacific Basin, it is also the site of United's Maintenance Operations Center.

United Airline's hundreds of planes fly thousands of passengers over millions of miles annually. Accomplishing these flights safely and on schedule requires that all United's aircraft be in top condition at all times. The Maintenance Operations Center (MOC) shoulders that responsibility, providing maintenance for the entire fleet of United aircraft.

The MOC is a huge facility of more than 3 million square feet of space covering 140 acres. Its five major departments for aircraft maintenance, engine and component maintenance, technical services, maintenance administration, and maintenance supply employ more than 9,000 mechanics, engineers, and other personnel. The MOC schedules aircraft inspections and overhauls for every aspect of the planes' maintenance, from flight instruments and avionics to carpeting and

seat covers in the cabins. Technicians in System Aircraft Maintenance Planning and Control (SAMPAC) coordinate communication between flight crews, engineering and maintenance personnel, and outside suppliers to solve maintenance problems. All aircraft maintenance and related activity is recorded in United's computerized aircraft maintenance-information system. This system also schedules and tracks service and keeps inventory of the MOC's aircraft components.

Not only does the MOC take care of the entire United fleet but it also

A Boeing 747 is gradually eased into its dock position for a heavy maintenance visit.

The largest of its kind in the world, United's Maintenance Operations Center employs more than 9,000 people and is the largest single employer in San Mateo County.

contracts with other international and domestic carriers to provide maintenance for their aircraft. In 1986 it handled the maintenance for more than 1,300 aircraft. Needless to say, the Maintenance Operations Center is the reason that United Airlines is the largest employer in San Mateo County.

Aircraft maintenance practices have changed markedly since the early days of United's predecessors. Early airline companies operated on shoestring budgets, and aircraft maintenance was much more haphazard in those days. In the 1920s Vern Gorst, proprietor of Pacific Air Transport, a future member of United Airlines, always kept an eye out for extra engines and plane parts at bargain prices. He filled bins in his hangar with these extra parts and used them to replace worn components in the planes. Walter Varney, founder of Varney Airlines—another predecessor of United—ran a flight school in San Mateo, and hired his school mechanics and students to repair and maintain his

planes.

Improvements in aircraft maintenance became necessary due in part to the technological advances that have made aircraft more powerful and complex. In the early days Varney airmail carriers were single-engine, 90-horsepower Swallow planes, which had a difficult time flying over mountains with a load of mailbags and a pilot. Today United flies an all-jet fleet of McDonnell Douglas DC-10s and DC-8s, as well as Boeing 727s, 737s, 747s, and 767s.

United actually originated from Varney Airlines, which began the first western commercial airline service in 1926 as an airmail carrier. Only a few weeks before, the San Francisco Airport—then known as Mills Field—had begun operations. Boeing Air Transport, a later merger of Varney, Pacific Air Transport, and National Air Transport, used the facilities for a short time.

The merged airlines of Boeing Transport were managed by United Airlines, created for that purpose in 1931. By this time United had originated stewardess service in the industry, when it hired eight women to serve on its route from Chicago to San Francisco. In 1932 the Pacific Air Transport division of United signed a contract with Mills Field and moved there for commercial operations.

Since its opening Mills Field management had been searching with great difficulty for major airline companies to operate from its facilities. The site was not satisfactory to many carriers, and competition was tough from the East Bay airports. Many airlines feared the airport facil-

ities were unsafe, and moved their operations across the bay. United was the first major airline to sign a contract with Mills, bringing more business to the airport.

This success was only temporary, for the deepening Depression had adverse effects on the airport's business. In 1934 the federal government cancelled all commercial

A view inside United's computerized engine test cell facility. Mechanics are able to monitor all aspects of an engine's performance from the control panel.

United overhauls and repairs more than 1,000 jet engines per year. Pictured is a General Electric CF6 engine used on DC-10 aircraft.

airmail contracts, which meant United was the only airmail carrier still in business. Two years later it was the only commercial air transport company operating out of San Francisco.

Although the Depression had deepened, United's activities continued unabated. The firm completed more than 14,000 arrivals and departures from San Francisco alone that year. That same year United began to install flight kitchens to prepare food for its passengers. In 1940 United signed its Maintenance Operations Center agreement with the San Francisco Airport, providing a huge boost to the local economy.

The Public Utilities Commission (PUC) praised the agreement, stating that it was "the greatest single industrial development in the history of the San Francisco Airport, and it will be an ever-expanding addition to the

commercial life of the city and community."

The PUC was right. Due to the establishment of the Maintenance Operations Center, United's expanded presence at the airport gave the postwar building boom great impetus. Employment with United and the airport contributed to the rapid population growth of the region.

United has been able to expand during its history through mergers such as the one with Capital Airlines in 1961. After suffering financial losses in the late 1960s and weathering the early days of airline deregulation, United grew dramatically again when it acquired Pan American World Airways' Pacific Division in 1985. This development made United a major international airline, as it acquired routes to Japan, Hong Kong, the People's Republic of China, Singapore, Korea, Thailand,

A time exposure presents molten slag as filaments of light during an inert gas welding operation. The mechanic is working on an internal oil sleeve from a turbine engine that powers the airline's wide-body aircraft.

Australia, New Zealand, and the Philippines. As the San Francisco International Airport has grown into a major transportation center, it has become one of the most important stations for United, from which the airline provides flights thoughout the increasingly important Pacific Region.

The company has been a leader in its field in a number of ways. Many aspects of commercial flight

A dramatic view shot from inside the exhaust funnel of the newest engine test cell at United Airlines' Maintenance Operations Center at San Francisco International Airport shows mechanics working on a General Electric CF6 turbine engine of the type that powers the Douglas DC-10 wide-body jetliner.

that we take for granted were initiated by United Airlines. It was the first airline to fly fare-paying passengers coast to coast. The first commercial flight of a Boeing 767 was completed by United Airlines from San Francisco in 1982. The carrier was the first to install automatic baggage conveyor systems at arrival gates. Before these conveyor systems were installed, all baggage was transferred from gates to planes by hand. United was also the first to use a nationwide computerized reservations system, which replaced a hand-sorted and -distributed reservations system.

Today United Airlines is the largest airline at the San Francisco International Airport, and one of the largest airlines in the world. Its Maintenance Operations Center and the continuing growth of the airline industry will continue to make United Airlines a very important aspect of the San Mateo County economy.

HISTORICAL OLD MOLLOY'S

Lanty Molloy has probably heard every cemetery joke in the book. He's the proprietor of Historical Old Molloy's, the only tavern in Colma, a central burial ground for the Bay Area for 100 years. Many of those who encountered Molloy's after a funeral have returned on happier occasions.

The tavern was, in fact, founded on the funeral business. Anticipating the role of Colma as a burial ground, Patrick Brooks built it as the Brooksville Hotel in 1883 to house the cemetery builders. Holy Cross Cemetery, first of the town's 11 cemeteries, opened in 1887 directly across the street.

By 1901 burials were forbidden in San Francisco because of high property values, and Colma's funeral business expanded. The Brooksville Hotel was always full of cemetery builders who found it easier to live at the hotel than to commute to and from Colma.

The Brooks left the establishment in 1912, although it remained part of their estate for many years.

During Prohibition the hotel was a lively speakeasy and a popular spot for patrons from nearby San Francisco, and it is reputed that the rooms upstairs sometimes housed ladies of the evening.

The Molloy family arrived on the scene in 1929. Frank Molloy was an Irishman from Donegal who had immigrated to San Francisco in 1905. After starting as a busboy, he became a tavern owner and real estate investor, and was once president of the United Irish Societies. He purchased the Brooksville from the Brooks estate in 1929, turning it over to a manager.

In 1937 Molloy decided to manage the Brooksville himself. He renamed it Molloy's Springs, and moved his family to Colma and into the hotel, where they lived until 1947.

While mourners continued to visit to drink a last farewell to departed friends and family, and others stopped in on occasion after visiting a grave (many arrived on the old 40 suburban streetcar line, which ran past the front door en

Frank Molloy, shown here with his wife, Martha, and four of his children, was proprietor of Molloy's Springs from 1927 to 1965. His son, Lanty, is the proprietor today.

route from San Francisco to San Mateo), Molloy's became the social hub of the community as tract after tract of the new post-World War II homes covered the old cabbage fields.

Returning from Army duty during the Korean War, Frank's son, Lanty, began taking over from his father and putting his own stamp on the place. He changed the name to Historical Old Molloy's and plastered the walls with his vast collection of historical photos and newspaper clippings, including one of the best collections of boxing photos around.

Because Colma has no parks and recreation department, Lanty Molloy's sometimes fills the role with annual chili cook-offs, Fourth of July parties, and a Haunted Mansion Halloween party co-sponsored by the city.

While mourners still drop in after burials, many other gatherings are common as well, with wedding receptions, banquets, birthday parties, and political gatherings often filling the back room. Grandson Francis Molloy handles the social calendar.

The raffish members of E. Clampus Vitus meet here every January to commemorate the 1880 death of Emperor Norton, once the self-proclaimed Emperor of the United States. More staid historical groups also gather at times, lured by the century-old building and its antiques.

Continuing the family tradition, several of Lanty's older sons tend bar from time to time, and the rest of the seven Molloy children help out with cleanup and on special occasions—there's no end in sight for the history of Molloy's.

Molloy's was originally built as the Brooksville Hotel to house the workers building the cemeteries of Colma.

SAN FRANCISCO AIRPORT HILTON

When the San Francisco Airport Hilton opened in 1959, it was one of the pioneers in the concept of airport hotels. Airline travel had become indispensable to the business world, and the airport was a prime spot at which to locate convenient, comfortable accommodations for the business traveler.

The Airport Hilton is almost 30 years old, but it has continued to change and grow to meet the ever-changing needs of its clientele. Although the hotel's main customer is the traveler, it has also continued to add new services that bring in patrons from the local community as well.

The San Francisco Airport Hilton, originally called the Hilton Inn, was the first of the Hilton chain's 36 air-

port hotels. A few years after its opening, another Hilton was built in downtown San Francisco, and the Hilton Inn took on its present name to differentiate the two.

Business hotels were much less luxurious accommodations than they are today. The Hilton Inn had 300 rooms, both hotel and motel style, and a coffee shop for its guests. For more formal dining, guests could go to the French Corner or to the International Club, a club and restaurant that leased space from the hotel. The restaurants and the club were also popular with local clientele. Elva Owsley, presently a hostess for the Hilton's Barronshire restaurant, was a novice waitress at the coffee shop in those early days and remembers it

was "always busy."

In 1968 the hotel expanded by adding 100 more rooms and changing over to a hotel-only format. It also leased space to a new club, Tiger-A-Go-Go. Complete with live bands and go-go girls, the club had patrons standing in line for hours to get in. Tiger-A-Go-Go was a short-lived feature of the hotel, soon replaced by entertainment more in keeping with the hotel's image.

The 1970s were a period of significant growth for the Hilton, especially in the area of food service. Although the hotel had once been a place to rest between flight connections, it was beginning to provide a greater range of services for many types of customers. In 1971 the establishment added a third floor, result-

Located on the San Francisco International Airport grounds, the aptly named San Francisco Airport Hilton is convenient to both the business traveler and local clientele.

ace, an annual rodeo event. Until 1976 the Airport Hilton purchased the grand champion steer from the show, and provided accommodations for the hundreds of participating cowboys. By 1977 enough hotels had been built closer to the Cow Palace that participants no longer had to travel as far as the airport for rooms.

The hotel has also hosted a number of important guests. Its Presidential Suite has accommodated political figures such as then-Governor Ronald Reagan, Walter Mondale, Mayor Tom Bradley of Los Angeles, and Senator Alan Cranston. Entertainers including Bill Cosby, Ike and Tina Turner, Clint Eastwood, and Vincent Price have also stayed at the hotel.

The Airport Hilton continues to remain competitive by reevaluating and improving its services. The management believes that the hotel's age should never dictate its image and is always working to keep the hotel fresh and up to date. For example, many rooms that once offered free coffee service now have private bars. To cater to the increasing fitness awareness of its guests, the hotel has an Olympic-size swimming pool and exercise rooms added in 1986. The importance of the business traveler is in evidence in the business services available. To provide an office away from the office, the Airport Hilton offers its Business Center—complete with a personal computer, facsimile, copier, and transcription services.

As the San Francisco Airport Hilton continues to improve its services and accommodations, the success of its ever-changing approach to the market is evident in the growth it has enjoyed. From its original 160 employees the hotel has doubled to 350 employees, more than half of whom are in the food services. The number of rooms has also doubled.

The hotel's location on the San Francisco International Airport grounds is an obvious asset, as travel continues to grow in popularity and importance in the business world.

ing in a total of 500 rooms. It also added new facilities to cater to the changing needs of the business traveler and local clientele. The French Corner was remodeled with a British motif and renamed the Barronshire after Barron Hilton, the son of the hotels' founder. The Tiger-A-Go-Go closed in 1972; shortly afterward the hotel began weighing a proposal for banquet facilities. After much consideration the management decided to build the International Ballroom where once was a putting green and a helicopter pad.

The 7,200-square-foot International Ballroom, one of the largest banquet rooms on the peninsula, opened in 1976. It was an immediate success. The ballroom provided space and catering service for classes, meetings, bar mitzvahs, and receptions—events that brought in both traveling and local clientele. Naturally, the increased clientele brought in by these affairs contributed to improved room occupancy.

The San Francisco Airport Hilton has hosted events of local and national significance. The hotel was the site of a press conference held for the American hostages returning from Iran. For many years the Hilton served as headquarters for the Grand National Show at the Cow Pal-

MOSS BEACH DISTILLERY

The Moss Beach Distillery is a seafood restaurant with a terrific view of the ocean, and is the first oyster bar on the San Mateo coast. Now a popular spot for romantic dining and Sunday brunches, it was once a favorite roadhouse of rumrunners, politicians, silent-film stars, and a ghost.

Frank Torres opened the restaurant in 1927 as Frank Torres' Marine View Hotel, where he served Peruvian dishes from his native country. During these Prohibition years the San Mateo coast was rampant with alcohol smuggling, as its protected coves and isolation provided cover from the law. Rumor has it that some of the contraband cargo ended up on the tables of Marine View patrons.

The Marine View became a place where the wealthy and the notorious could enjoy their vices in relative safety. The downstairs rooms and a bordello next door provided other comforts for patrons. The Marine View even had a large garage that allowed its visitors to drive in unseen and enter by the back stairs.

During the raucous period the death of a young lady in blue triggered the ghost stories that have accompanied the restaurant's history ever since. Her body was found on the beach below, and rumor has it that she was a young prostitute from next door, or possibly the victim of a love triangle. Her ghost, known as The Blue Lady, has appeared at the restaurant repeatedly over the years.

Frank ran the Marine View for about 20 years before turning it over to his son, Victore "Vic" Torres. The new owner changed the name to Vic Torres' Marine View Hotel, and installed brightly colored stained-glass windows with panes framed by his name. Vic had commissioned Otto Dressler, a San Francisco artist, to design three more windows portraying wine, women, and song, but died before he was able to install them. Shortly afterward the old bordello buildings next door burned down, closing a fast and furious era in the history of Moss Beach.

Mike Murphy was the next proprietor. He renamed the hotel the Galway Bay Inn, after a famous bay in Ireland. He served steak, seafood, and the specialty of the house—Gaelic coffee. Overnight accommodations were still available, although the company provided in Frank Torres' day was no longer included.

Murphy left in 1973. Then Dave and Patricia Andrews, an architect and an artist from Southern Califor-

Moss Beach Distillery is located in what was the notorious Marine View Hotel in the 1920s when this photograph was taken. Courtesy, **Half Moon Bay Memories, The Coastside's Colorful Past** *by June Morrall Moonbeam Press, 1978*

nia, heard about the place from a friend and decided to take on the challenge of running an oceanside restaurant. With much help from friends, the Andrews were able to reopen the restaurant as the Moss Beach Distillery.

While retaining the original design of the restaurant, the Andrews changed the menu to provide elegant seafood dining. They hope to restore many of the architectural features of the original building, and have reproduced Frank Torres' Marine View dishes for the table settings. They've added some new features as well, such as Sunday brunch and Sunday jazz concerts.

The clientele today is largely local, and the pleasures they seek here are perfectly legal. Still, one of the old-timers keeps coming back. The Blue Lady stops in now and then to remind the Moss Beach Distillery of the wild, old days.

Friends and relatives of the participants and polo enthusiasts watch a match from the veranda of the Carolan Clubhouse at Crossways Farm in Burlingame, sometime in the late nineteenth century. Courtesy, The Bartlett Collection, San Mateo County Historical Association Archives

Above: *By the turn of the century the street-car line extended south down the Peninsula to San Mateo, where it terminated. This line continued to operate until the the 1940s. Students from San Francisco and the North County traveled by streetcar to San Mateo to attend the area's first junior college. Courtesy, San Mateo County Historical Association Archives*

Left: *Members of the Bay Area Wheelers pose with their cycles on the beach at Coyote Point in central San Mateo County in the late 1900s. Courtesy, San Mateo County Historical Association Archives*

Patrons

The following individuals, companies, and organizations have made a valuable commitment to the quality of this publication. Windsor Publications and the San Mateo County Historical Association gratefully acknowledge their participation in *Peninsula Portrait: An Illustrated History of San Mateo County.*

Ampex Corporation*
Bay City Flower Company*
Bay Meadows Racetrack*
Bay View Federal Savings and Loan Association*
David D. Bohannon Organization*
Borel Bank & Trust Company*
Burlingame Bank & Trust Co.*
Burlingame Public Library
California Water Service Company
Camsco Produce Company*
City of San Mateo
Cotchett & Illston*
Cunha's Country Store*
De Monet Industries*
First American Title Insurance Company*
Gelsar*
Genentech, Inc.*
Daniel C. Gilbrech
Historical Old Malloy's*
History, Arts and Science Commission of Daly City
Brian G. Kestner
Lincoln Property Company*
Menlo Park Historical Association
Moss Beach Distillery*
Mr. & Mrs. John F. O'Connell
Pacific Gas and Electric Company*
Pearson, Del Prete & Co.
The Peninsula Regent*
Port of Redwood City
Redwood Shores, Inc.*

San Francisco Airport Hilton*
San Mateo County Convention and Visitors Bureau
San Mateo County Economic Development Association*
San Mateo County Genealogical Society
San Mateo County Library
Sunset Magazine*
The *Times* (The *San Mateo Times*)*
Town of Colma
United Airlines*
G.W. Williams Co.

* Partners in Progress *Peninsula Portrait: An Illustrated History of San Mateo County.* The histories of these companies and organizations appear in Chapter 7, beginning on page 107.

BIBLIOGRAPHY

1. Books

Bancroft, Hubert Howe. *History of California.* San Francisco: The History Company, 1886.

Bean, Walton. *California: an Interpretive History.* New York: McGraw-Hill, 1968.

Boneu, F. Companys. *Gaspar de Portola: Explorer and Founder of California.* Spain: Instituto de Estudios Ilerdenses, 1983.

Brown, Alan K. *Sawpits in the Spanish Red Woods: 1787-1849.* San Mateo: San Mateo County Historical Assoc., 1966.

Chandler, Samuel C. *Gateway to the Peninsula.* Daly City: City of Daly City, 1973.

Cloud, Roy W. *History of San Mateo County.* Chicago: S.J. Clarke Publishing Co., 1928.

Flynn, William. *Men, Money and Mud: The Story of San Francisco International Airport.* San Francisco: San Francisco International Airport, 1954.

Heizer, Robert F. *The Costanoan Indians.* Cupertino: California History Center, 1974.

Hynding, Alan. *From Frontier to Suburb.* Belmont: Star Publishing Company, 1982.

Japanese American Citizens League, San Mateo Chapter. *1872-1942: A Community Story.* San Mateo: San Mateo Chapter JACL, 1981.

Kaufman, Linda. *South San Francisco.* South San Francisco: Linda Kaufman, 1976.

Krober, Alfred L. *Handbook of the Indians of California.* Washington: U.S. Government Printing Office, 1925.

Margolin, Malcolm. *The Ohlone Way.* Berkeley: Heyday Books, 1978.

Mora, Jo. *Californios.* Garden City: Doubleday & Company, Inc., 1949.

Morrall, June. *Half Moon Bay Memories.* El Granada: Moonbeam Press, 1978.

Postel, Mitchell. *History of the Burlingame Country Club.* Hillsborough: Burlingame Country Club, 1982.

Regnery, Dorothy F. *The Battle of Santa Clara.* San Jose: Smith and McKay Printing Company, 1978.

Richards, Gilbert. *Crossroads.* Woodside: Gilbert Richards Publications, 1973.

Ringler, Donald P. *San Mateo-USA: The Golden Years.* San Mateo: City of San Mateo, 1975.

Ringler, Donald P. and George Rossi. *Filoli.* Hillsborough: Private printing, 1978.

Shumate, Albert. *The Notorious I.C. Woods of the Adams Express.* Glendale: Arthur H. Clark Company, 1986.

Simon, Barbara. *A New Town Comes of Age: Foster City, California.* Foster City: Foster City Chamber of Commerce, 1985.

Stanger, Frank M. *History of San Mateo County.* San Mateo: A.H. Cawston, 1938.

Stanger, Frank M. *Peninsula Community Book.* San Mateo: A.H. Cawston, 1946.

Stanger, Frank M. *South From San Francisco.* San Mateo: San Mateo County Historical Assoc., 1963.

Stanger, Frank M. *Sawmills in the Redwoods.* San Mateo: San Mateo County Historical Assoc., 1967.

Stanger, Frank M. and Alan K. Brown. *Who Discovered the Golden Gate?* San Mateo: San Mateo County Historical Assoc., 1969.

Storer, Tracy I. and Loyd P. Tevis, Jr. *California Grizzly.* Berkeley: University of California Press, 1955.

Strobridge, William F. *Golden Gate to Golden Horn.* San Mateo: San Mateo County Historical Assoc., 1973.

Unknown Author. *History of San Mateo County.* San Francisco: B.F. Alley, 1883.

Wagner, Jack R. *The Last Whistle.* Berkeley: Howell-North Books, 1974.

Watkins, C. Malcolm. *The White House of Half Moon Bay.* Half Moon Bay: Johnston House Foundation, 1972.

2. Articles

Brown, Alan K. "Indians of San Mateo County." San Mateo: *La Peninsula,* San Mateo County Historical Assoc. (Winter, 73-74).

Chandler, Sam. "The Colma Cemetery Complex." San Mateo: *La Peninsula,* San Mateo County Historical Assoc. (Spring, 1979).

Drye, Shirley. "Don Francisco Sanchez—A Man of Integrity." San Mateo: *La Peninsula,* San Mateo County Historical Assoc. (January, 1986).

Fredricks, Darold E. "The City of San Bruno: A Look to the Past." San Mateo: *La Peninsula,* San Mateo County Historical Assoc. (December, 1984).

Guest, Francis F. "The Habit of Affection: Pastoral Theology, Padres and Indians." San Francisco: *The Californians* (September/October, 1984).

Guido, Francis. "The 40 Line." South San Francisco: *The Western Railroader* (March, 1975).

Harris, Audrey E. "The History of Millbrae." San Mateo: *La Peninsula,* San Mateo County Historical Assoc. (February, 1972).

Hills, Ernest. "Stagecoach History in San Mateo County." San Mateo: *La Peninsula,* San Mateo County Historical Assoc. (May, 1956).

Leon-Portilla, Miquel. "Fray Francisco Palou: Serra's First Biographer." San Francisco: *The Californians* (September/October, 1984).

Levy, Richard. "Costanoan." *Handbook of North American Indians* (vol. 8), Washington: Smithsonian Institution (1978). Robert F. Heizer, volume editor.

Lummis, Keith. "As the Padre Saw It." San Francisco: *The Californians* (September/October, 1984).

Postel, Mitchell. "More Than A Grain." San Mateo: *La Peninsula,* San Mateo County Historical Assoc. (Winter, 1976).

Postel, Mitchell. "San Mateo County Historical Association 1935-1985." San Mateo: *La Peninsula,* San Mateo County Historical Assoc. (May, 1985).

Ringler, Donald P. "Hillsborough-San Mateo Mansions." San Mateo: *La Peninsula,* San Mateo County Historical Assoc. (Winter, 1976).

Sears, Betty. "The Not-So-Dry Years." San Mateo: *La Peninsula,* San Mateo County Historical Assoc. (Summer, 1980).

Stanger, Frank M. "The Hospice or Mission San Mateo." San Francisco: *California Historical Society Quarterly* (September, 1944).

Stanger, Frank M. "The Grizzlies Were Here." San Mateo: *La Peninsula,* San Mateo County Historical Assoc. (February, 1949).

Stanger, Frank M. "Redwood City." San Mateo: *La Peninsula,* San Mateo County Historical Assoc. (October, 1951).

Stanger, Frank M. "Redwood City Centennial Edition." San Mateo: *La Peninsula,* San Mateo County Historical Assoc. (May, 1967).

Still, Mark. "Coastal Whaling: Mainstay of Fashion." San Mateo: *La Peninsula,* San Mateo County Historical Assoc. (September, 1983).

Thomas, Ealine. "The Italians in San Mateo County" and "Leonetto Cipriani—The Count of Belmont." San Mateo: *La Peninsula,* San Mateo County Historical Assoc. (Fall, 1981).

3. Manuscripts

Dunbar, Patricia L. "The Portuguese Migration to the Coastside of San Mateo County." Archives of San Mateo County Historical Assoc., 1977.

Jensen, M. "An Outline History of Lawndale." Archives of San Mateo County Historical Assoc., 1937.

Postel, Mitchell. "Vigil on the Golden Gate: The Environmental History of the San Francisco Bay Since 1850." Archives of San Mateo County Historical Museum, 1977.

Postel, Mitchell. "Legacy of a Lost Resource: San Mateo County's Bayline Industries." Archives of San Mateo County Historical Assoc., 1987.

INDEX